Please Help Us Frogs...

Do You Know How To Care For A Pet Frog?

Most frogs have teeth, although usually only on their upper jaw. The teeth are used to hold prey in place until the frog can swallow it.

The biggest frog in the world is the Goliath frog. It lives in West Africa and can measure more than a foot in length and weigh more than 7 pounds - as much as a newborn baby.

There's a type of poison dart frog called the blue-jeans frog. It has a red body with blue legs. It is also sometimes called the strawberry dart frog.

The red-eyed tree frog lays it eggs on the underside of leaves that hang over water. When the eggs hatch, the tadpoles fall into the water below.

A group of birds is called a flock, a group of cattle is called a herd, but a group of frogs is called an army.

The glass frog has translucent skin, so you can see its internal organs, bones and muscles through its skin. You can even observe its heart beating and its stomach digesting food.

There is a frog in Indonesia that has no lungs - it breathes entirely through its skin.

The waxy monkey frog secretes a wax from its neck and uses its legs to rub that wax all over its body. The wax prevents the skin of the frog from drying out in sunlight.

When Darwin's frog tadpoles hatch, a male frog swallows the tadpoles. He keeps the tiny amphibians in his vocal sac for about 60 days to allow them to grow. He then proceeds to cough up tiny, fully formed frogs.

When a frog swallows its prey, it blinks, which pushes its eyeballs down on top of the mouth to help push the food down its throat.

The wood frog of North America actually freezes in the winter and is reanimated in the spring. When temperatures fall, the wood frog's body begins to shut down, and its breathing, heartbeat and muscle movements stop.
The water in the frog's cells freezes and is replaced with glucose and urea to keep cells from collapsing.

When there's a thaw, the frog's warms up, its body functions resume and it hops off like nothing ever happened.

When Darwin's frog tadpoles hatch, a male frog swallows the tadpoles. He keeps the tiny amphibians in his vocal sac for about 60 days to allow them to grow. He then proceeds to cough up tiny, fully formed frogs.

When a frog swallows its prey, it blinks, which pushes its eyeballs down on top of the mouth to help push the food down its throat.

The wood frog of North America actually freezes in the winter and is reanimated in the spring. When temperatures fall, the wood frog's body begins to shut down, and its breathing, heartbeat and muscle movements stop. The water in the frog's cells freezes and is replaced with glucose and urea to keep cells from collapsing.

One gram of the toxin produced by the skin of the golden poison dart frog could kill 100,000 people.

The female Surinam toad lays up to 100 eggs, which are then distributed over her back. Her skin swells around the eggs until they become embedded in a honeycomb-like structure. After 12 to 20 weeks, fully formed young toads emerge by pushing out through the membrane covering the toad's back.

A frog completely sheds its skin about once a week. After it pulls off the old, dead skin, the frog usually eats it.

Pacific tree frog is the frog that says "Ribbit!" So it's the one we hear in the background in movies and on TV.

The smallest frogs are the gold frog of Brazil and a frog from Cuba, just discovered in 1996, which doesn't have an English name yet. Both these frogs are less than one centimetre long. Hardly bigger are some of the poison frogs.

The world's tiniest frogs are smaller than a dime, and the largest frog can grow to be longer than a foot and weigh more than 7 pounds!

Most frogs and toads breathe (and take in moisture) through their skin through a process called cutaneous gas exchange, but they also have lungs with which they breathe. During the time they stay submerged under water or buried in soil (such as during hibernation) they ONLY breathe through their skin.

Frogs' ears are specially "tuned" to absorb the mid-point of the pitch of the call of their particular species. For example, ears of female Spring Peepers are specifically tuned to absorb the mid-point of the pitch of the male Peeper's call.

Spring peepers are one of the first frog species to start calling in the Eastern U.S. and Canada in the spring. These tiny frogs are less than 1 1/4 inches in length. Because they are so small, peepers are nearly impossible to see, yet they can ALWAYS be heard whenever they're singing. The voice of one peeper sounds like a short, high-pitched whistle.
But when a group of spring peepers is calling together they sound like jingle bells on a winter sleigh.

Pipa pipa, carries her young embedded in the skin of her back. After mating, the eggs sink gradually into the female's back, and a skin pad forms over the eggs. The developing juvenile frogs are visible inside their pockets for several days before hatching.

They emerge over a period of days, thrusting their head and forelegs out first and then struggling free.

The gastric brooding frog of Australia swallows her fertilized eggs. The tadpoles remain in her stomach for up to eight weeks, finally hopping out of her mouth as little frogs. During the brooding period, gastric secretions cease otherwise she would digest her own offspring.

Among Darwin frogs, it is the male who swallows and stores the developing tadpoles in his vocal sac until juvenile frogs emerge.

The Australian water-holding frog is a desert dweller that can wait up to seven years for rain. It burrows underground and surrounds itself in a transparent cocoon made of its own shed skin.

Frogs are freshwater creatures, although some frogs such as the Florida leopard frog are able to live in brackish or nearly completely salt waters.

Almost all frogs fertilize the eggs outside of the female's body.

The marsupial frog keeps her eggs in a pouch like a kangaroo. When the eggs hatch into tadpoles, she opens the pouch with her toes and spills them into the water.

Like all amphibians, frogs are cold-blooded, meaning their body temperatures change with the temperature of their surroundings.

When temperatures drop, some frogs dig burrows underground or in the mud at the bottom of ponds. They hibernate in these burrows until spring, completely still and scarcely breathing.

The wood frog can live north of the Arctic Circle, surviving for weeks with 65 per cent of its body frozen. This frog uses glucose in its blood as a kind of antifreeze that concentrates in its vital organs, protecting them from damage while the rest of the body freezes solid.

To blend into the environment, the Budgett's frog is muddy brown in colour, while the Vietnamese mossy frog has spotty skin and bumps to make them look like little clumps of moss or lichen.

Many poisonous frogs, such as the golden poison frog and dyeing poison frog, are boldly coloured to warn predators of their dangerous toxic skins.

Although their skins are not toxic, these mimics may gain protection from predators by looking dangerous.

Like all amphibians, frogs are cold-blooded, meaning their body temperatures change with the temperature of their surroundings.

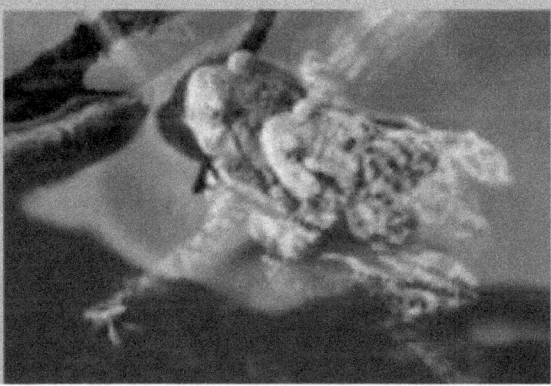

Frogs have excellent night vision and are very sensitive to movement. The bulging eyes of most frogs allow them to see in front, to the sides, and partially behind them. When a frog swallows food, it pulls its eyes down into the roof of its mouth, to help push the food down its throat.

Frogs were the first land animals with vocal cords. Male frogs have vocal sacs-pouches of skin that fill with air. Some frog sounds can be heard from a mile away.

Launched by their long legs, many frogs can leap more than 20 times their body length.

The Costa Rican flying tree frog soars from branch to branch with the help of its feet. Webbing between the frog's fingers and toes extends out, helping the frog glide.

There is evidence that frogs have roamed the Earth for more than 200 million years, at least as long as the dinosaurs.

The world's largest frog is the goliath frog of West Africa-it can grow to 15 inches and weigh up to 7 pounds.

One of the smallest is the Cuban tree toad, which grows to half an inch long.

While the life spans of frogs in the wild are unknown, frogs in captivity have been known to live more than 20 years.

There are over 6,000 species of frogs worldwide. Scientists continue to search for new ones.

Why Frogs Rock...?

What Frogs Handsome Enough To Kiss?

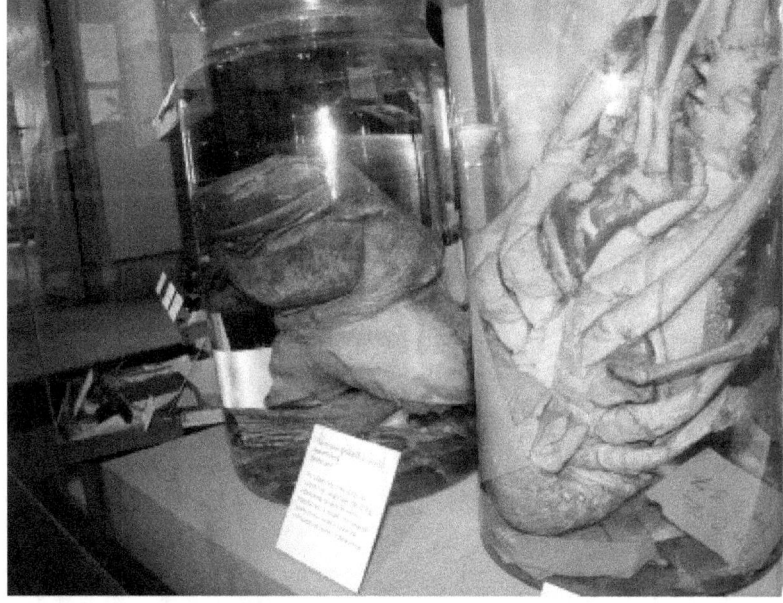

Weirdest Looking Toads & Frogs...

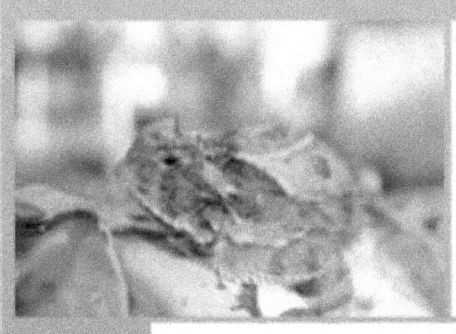

Fly Catching...!

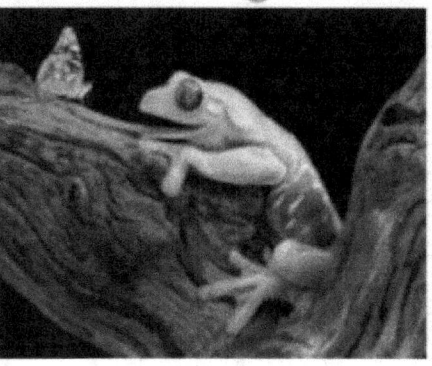
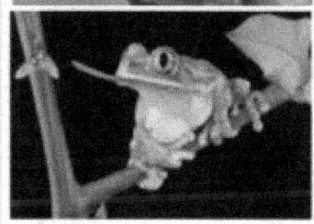
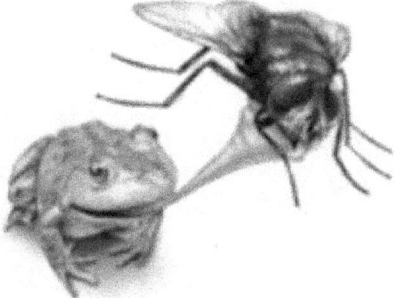

What Is Hibernation?

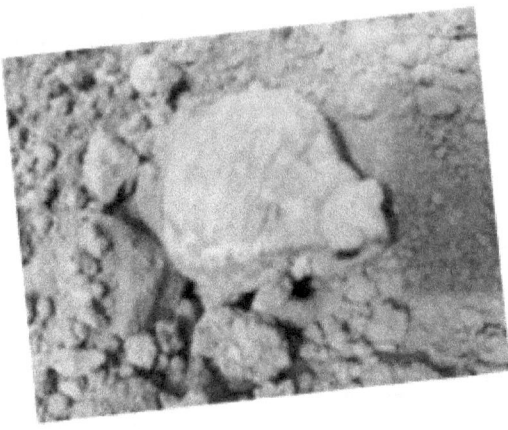

Every different species of frog makes its own special sound and it is only the male frog that can croak. They have a small sac in their throats that vibrates the air as they slowly let it out.

NPS Photo by James H. Evans, 1999

Frog Mating & Reproduction...

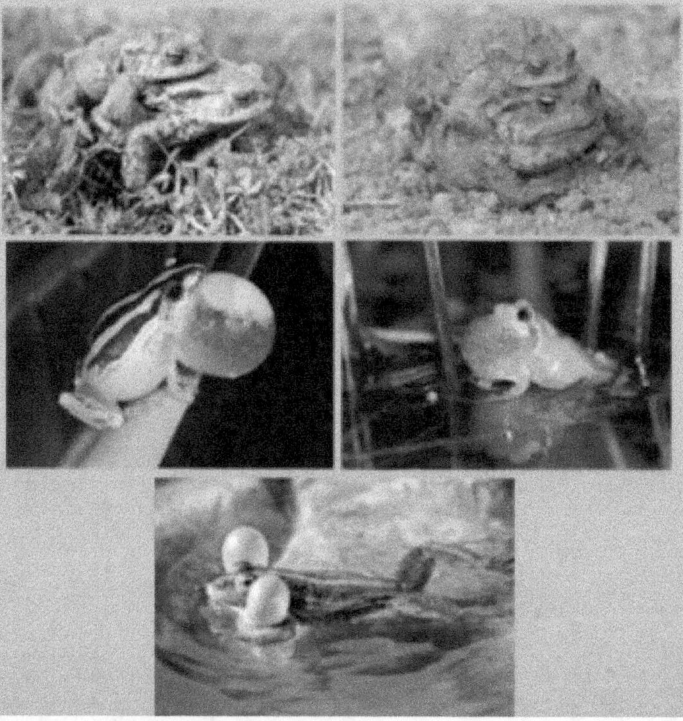

Frogs lay eggs in water which are
later hatched in tadpoles...

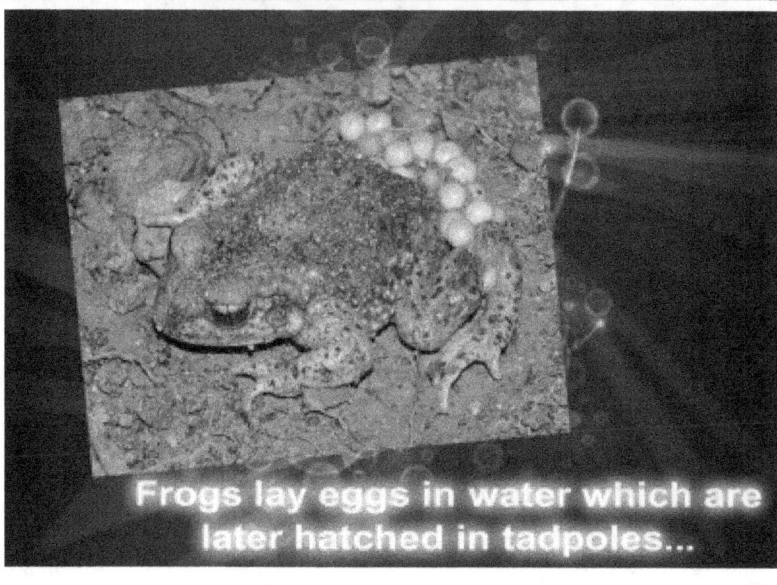

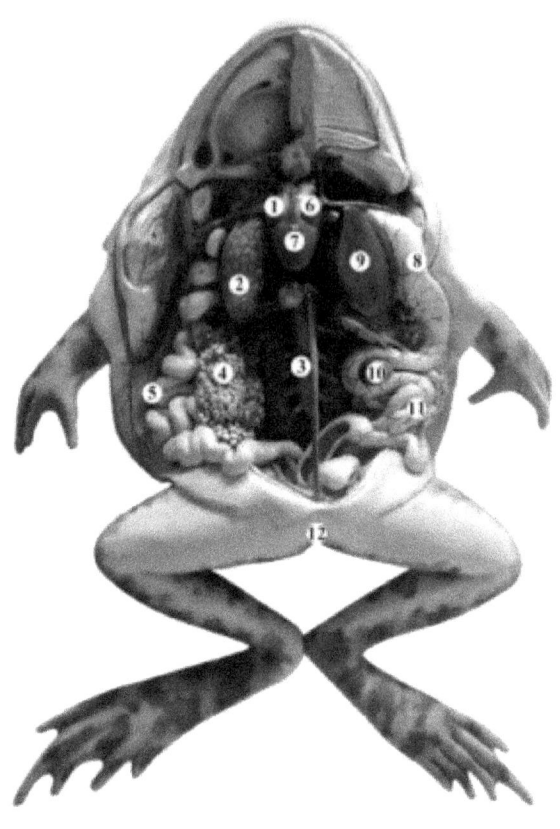

Source: Picture taken by Jonathan McIntosh
Frog anatomy display in NMH Washington DC, US

Frog Body System...

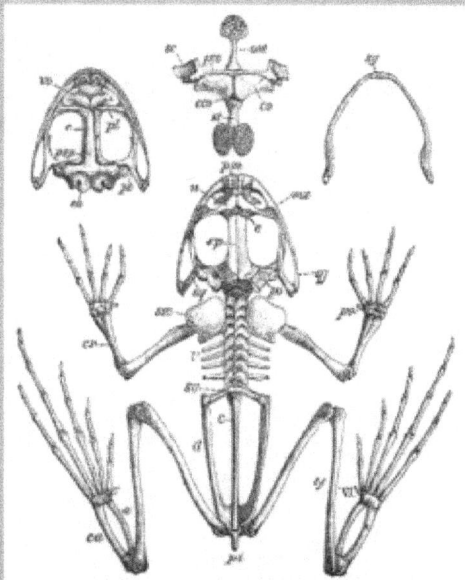

Skeleton of *Rana esculenta*. (Guide to Reptile Gallery B.M.)

- a. Astragalus.
- c. Coccyx.
- ca. Calcaneum.
- co. Cornoid.
- cr. Radius-ulna.
- e. Ethmoid.
- ec. Epicoracoid.
- eo. Exoccipital.
- fp. Frontoparietal.
- il. Ilium.
- mx. Maxillary.
- n. Nasal.
- ost. Ososternum.
- pco. Precoracoid.
- pl. Palatine.
- pi. Pubis-ischium.
- pm. Premaxillary.
- po. Prootic.
- po'. Pollex.
- psp. Parasphenoid.
- pt. Pterygoid.
- tj. Quadratojugal.
- sc. Scapula.
- sq. Squamosal.
- su. Suprascapula.
- st. Sternum.
- sv. Sacral vertebra.
- sy. Symphysial.
- tf. Tibia-fibula.
- v. Dorsal vertebra.
- vo. Vomer.
- VI. Rudiment of sixth toe.

Frogs Around The Globe...

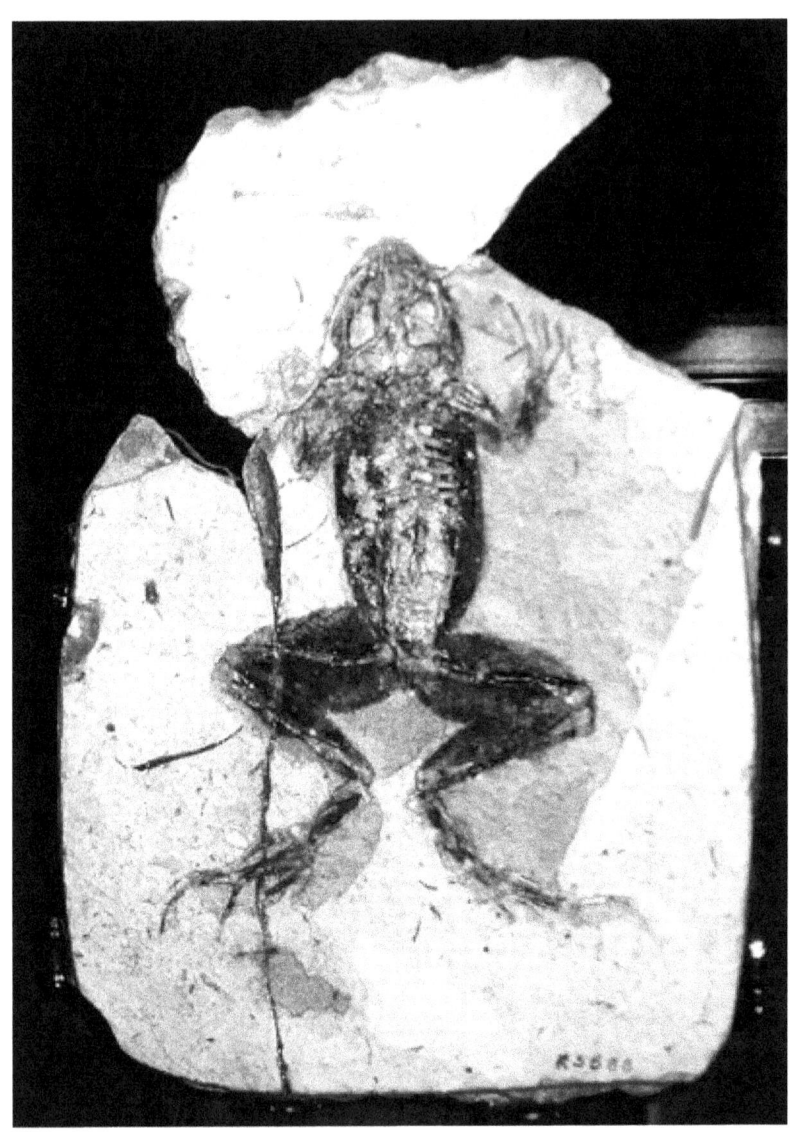

"Never try to catch two frogs with one hand" - Chinese Proverb

You can't tell by looking at a frog how high he will jump.

This is a work of fiction. Similarities to real people, places, or events are entirely coincidental.

FROGS AND TOADS DISCOVERY: FROG PICTURE BOOK FOR KIDS WITH FUN PHOTOS & ILLUSTRATIONS

First edition. July 4, 2017.

Copyright © 2017 Kate Cruso.

ISBN: 978-1386705772

Written by Kate Cruso.

My Favorite Quote About Frogs

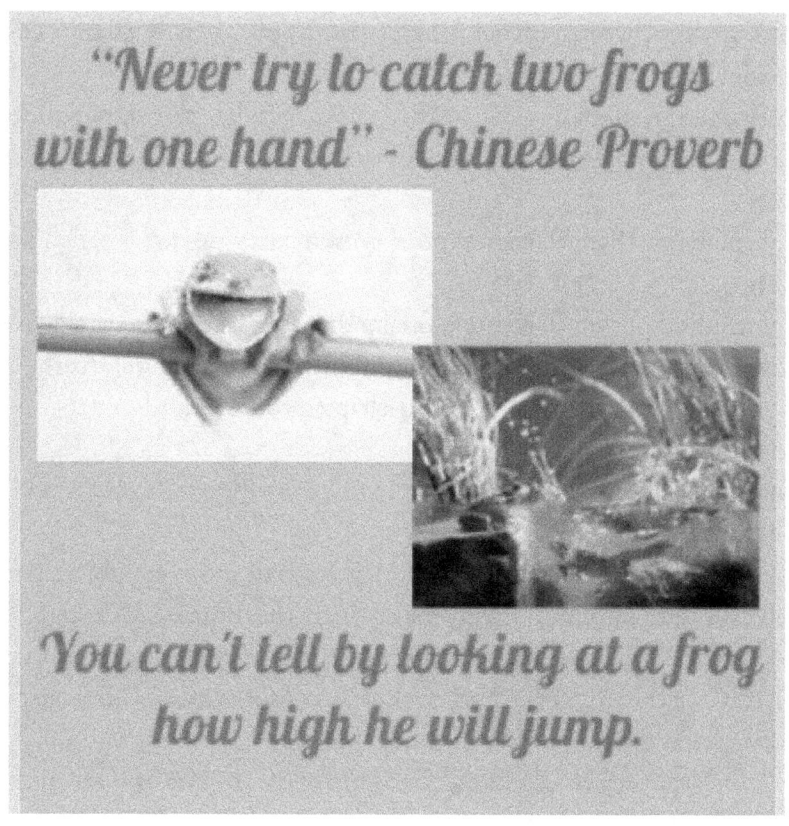

Introduction

The reason why I wrote this sea frog discover book as part of my "Discover Book Series" is an important one.

Every child should know about the issues that relate to frogs because frogs are a keystone group in the food web dynamics of many of the world's ecosystems.

Did you know that there is a type of poison dart frog that is called the blue jeans frog?

You will find out more of these fascinating frog facts and curious frog stories in the chapter that talks about some amazing frog revelations, truths & other curious stuff about frogs and in this chapter you will find out the ultimate answers about your frog questions.

Once your kid has gone through the discovery book, he or she will agree that frogs truly rock!

The fact that frogs are 265 million years old and were able to survive through evolution until today truly makes them the ultimate rock star!

It is true the frog is one of the most ancient species on the globe, but sadly enough some of the frog species are declining and some species are even considered endangered today.

In a concerted effort we must all be aware of the decline of some of the frog species and help to save them!

This book will provide your child with all the facts, stories, and pictures that are related to the world of frogs. Having a better understanding of who the frogs really are, from where they come, and how they relates to us humans.

It is important for your child to understand how frogs help balance the ecosystem that humans, plants, and animals live in.

Once your child does understand all these relationships, he or she will be able to have a better appreciation of frogs and of animals in general.

Your child will also discover many interesting, curious, and intriguing facts about frogs which will in turn help your child appreciate a frog's existence.

After having read the book your child will be better able to understand why frogs are so precious to us humans and why we need to save their heritage.

By reading the book your child will personally get in touch with some amazing frog moments and this alone is worth going through the discovery phase that this book is going to provide your child with.

In the end your child will know more cool things about frogs and this knowledge will enrich your child on a mental level because knowledge is power.

If your child is an informed kid, he or she knows more stuff which in turn will enable him or her to get into a deeper discovery process and this in turn will help raise your child's interest level making him or her more involved and engaged in life in general.

This active mental discovery process will ultimately lead to a higher intelligence level.

Once your child is knowledgeable about the species of frogs, he or she can decide which way to go from here and he or she can truly start a positive mental relationship and friendship with this cute and peaceful swimming, jumping, hibernating, digging, running, and locomoting animal.

Who knows but maybe this information is going to be the basis for some of your kid's future initiatives. Based on information like this your child might engage his or her initiative for the cause of sea turtles or any other endangered animals at a later point in time.

Helping shape a positive future and helping shape the intelligence of responsible individuals who are going to care for extinct animals and who might one day bring their own resourcefulness, responsibility, and initiative to the table is part of the reason why I made it my mission to create this discovery series.

This frog discovery book is the fourth volume within this discovery book series.

As a mother of twin boys and a little girl, I know that I want to be actively involved in their educational process to help shape their visions, imaginations, dreams, hopes, creativity, and their positive involvement with everything that this beautiful world of ours has to offer.

I have set my goal to help kids envision and discover intriguing, amazing, and curious stuff that they find cool and that is part of our life here on earth.

Encouraging them to view life from a totally new perspective and dimension helps kids build new mental connections between things that they might not have considered before is what I want to achieve with my books that I am writing for children about animals, nature, space, and other related issues.

Going through such an active discovery process helps stimulate the active thinking and contemplation process which in turn increases a child's intelligence in general.

Involving your child with a positive, creative, mentally involving and stimulating, interactive, and responsive educational discovery process where your kid gets satisfactory answers back is how you help shape the intelligence of your child.

If you are letting your child explore new and cool things about a subject you are making an active contribution into your child's future! Such an investment into your child's future is the most valuable investment that you can ever provide your child with.

This book will empower your child to raise and get answers for questions like why some frog species are endagnered, why the frog is such an amazing animal, why it is important to save the frog, what your child can do to help the endangered frog species, and lots more.

These are just some more additional reasons why this frog discovery book provides such an important contribution into your child's educational process and mental development.

Once your child is aware about all these issues that surround the frog, he or she will feel more enriched and in tune with the nature, the world of the animals, our environment, and our earth.

Helping to protect the valuable species that have been brought to us by mother nature is one of our priorities as human beings.

We as human beings can create a healthy balance and we as human beings have the intelligence to create a balanced, protected, happy and peaceful life between humans and animals happen.

As you can see there are many reasons why reading this frog discovery book is an important step into the future of your child.

I wrote the book in the most positive spirit and my main goal for the book can be summarized as follows.

As a mother it is my responsibility to entertain and engage my kids with positive educational content. In my opinion as a former first grade teacher, mother nature provides the richest sources of valuable content for a child. Human beings, animals, and plants are a good way to get your child started with the discovery process.

My kids always tell me that they love to be entertained while they discover something new at the same time. Learning about some cool new information is how they learn best and they love to consume a mixture of pictures, funny facts, stories, and the curious and intriguing side of a specific animal or topic that they are learning about.

I know from my own experience as an educator and researcher and from my interaction with children in general that kids love to learn stuff the cool way.

I listened to kids and took the responses that I got from them and it is my goal to surprise them with a real cool book series. This discovery book series is basically inspired by kids. It is made from kids for kids. It respects the way kids like to learn.

I created this book series in a way that respects the way how kids like to learn because they told me what they find cool and groovy and I listened to them and included it.

The book contains lots of pictures, cool facts, and other curious and intriguing stuff that kids just seem to be fascinated with.

This specific discovery book is about frogs and therefore it fulfills a second big goal. This book can also be seen as a contribution to help endangered frogs and to help stimulate children to contemplate about the endangered species of frogs.

This book should raise awareness about this endangered species in the eyes of a child. It should help a child be aware that it is possible between humans to sustainably coexist with frogs.

Lastly, I want to stress that this book is there to enrich your child's spirit, imagination, creativity, hope, dreams, and vision about the wonderful world of frogs.

A child must know that he or she has a stake in such a global cause like frogs.

Reading about today's issues in such a positive and mentally stimulating way helps empower a kid's creativity, initiative, and interaction to create a better and happier future for a life in balance with the nature.

A child should also know that although the situation of the frogs is very delicate, there are positive news in regards to the recovery process of declining frog species because there are human beings who act in a very responsible way that help frogs to sustain themselves in the nature by extending the nature reserves and by developing new projects and frog breeding and frog protection programs in a concerted effort to sustainably co exist and live in balance together with this endangered species - the cute tiny froggies!

This is the result of joint effort between the Amphibian Ark to help save more than 6,000 species of amphibians from disappearing by starting captive breeding programs, some responsive governments and local communities and their initiatives, and a group of responsible people like you and your child!

I truly hope that you and your child are going to enjoy the concept and the content of this book and I hope you get lots of valuable moments out of this discovery series.

I welcome every parent and child to discover the wonderful world of frogs - one of the oldest and most ancient species on earth, but sadly enough a declining and endangered species at the same time!

What Is The History Of Frogs? What Is Their Origin?

The Green Tree Frog of Today (only one of our many 4800 species)...but we are very ancient
creatures and our heritage goes 265 Million Years back in time...

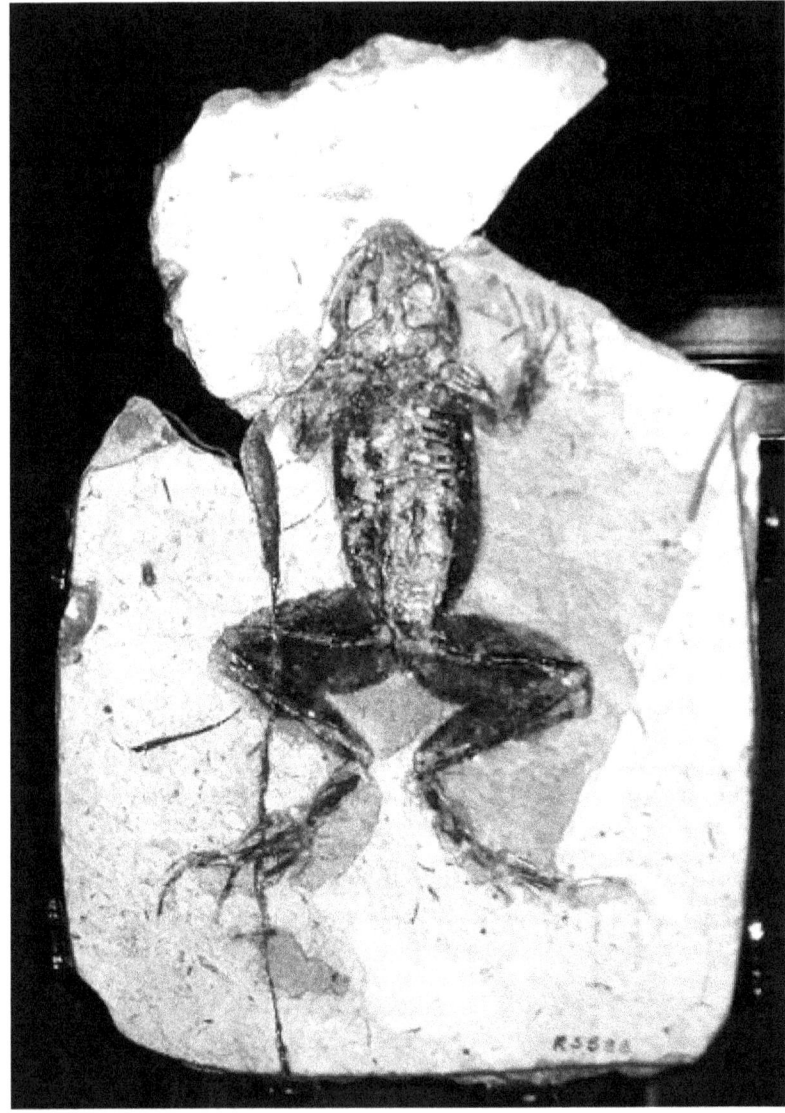

Source: Ghedoghedo - Fossil of Rana pueyoi, an extinct frog
This photo was taken in the Natural History Museum, London

Source: Kevin Walsh from Oxford, England
A fossilized frog, from Bechlejovice in
the Czech Republic

Did you know that the word frog comes from Anura (Ancient Greek an = the word: without and the word: oura = tail).

Researches found out about our ancestors that the oldest fossil (the protofrog) appeared in the early Triassic of Madagascar.

Other researchers and methods of research suggest that our origins extend further back and well into the Permian period which is 265 million years ago others say we are around 125 million years old and that we evolved after amphibians left the sea.

Amphibians left the sea around 360 million years ago to live on the land.

As we frogs and other amphibians moved to the land, we had to adapt ouselves in many ways and thus acquired features of both water and land animals.

Yes, we frogs have come a long way and we are a bunch of ancient and wise creatrues that have been able to adapt and survive until today.

Today, we frogs are widely distributed around the world. We are ranging from the tropics to the subarctic regions.

The largest and greatest concentration of our species diversity and population is found in beautiful tropical rainforests.

We frogs are a widely distributed animal and we are ranging from the tropics to the subarctic regions, however, the greatest concentration of our species and diversity is found in tropical rainforests.

Today, there are approximately 4,800 recorded species of us around the globe which accounts for over 85% of extant amphibian species.

We are also one of the 5 most diverse vertebrate orders.

Experts and researchers who have studies ancient animals like us a lot are saying that Amphibians like us were the first vertebrates that left the water to live on land.

Modern amphibians are called Lissamphibians (which include us frogs, toads, salamanders, newts)

The rare earthworm-like amphibians are called "caecilians" and they are believed to have radiated from a common ancestor.

What Are The Differences Between Frogs & Toads

What is the difference between us frogs and toads?

We frogs usually have a smooth, slimy, and moist skin. We spend most of our lives in or near the water. We frogs have strong, long legs, webbed hind feet, and two bulging eyes. We frogs lay eggs in masses, whereas toads usually lay eggs in long chains.

We frogs sometimes have upper teeth whereas toads have no teeth at all. Toads usually have a dry, warty looking skin and spend more time living on land than us frogs. Toads have stubby bodies with short hind legs.

Australian Green Tree Frog

Yes, we frogs are a diverse and largely carnivorous group of short-bodied, tailless amphibian creatures. We are composing the order of Anura

(Ancient Greek an- means without + oura means tail).

Janekpfeifer at de.wikipedia - Common Toads during migration in the Portuguese national park of Peneda-Gerês.

Source: Marek Szczepanek - another type of toad

Where Are Frogs Found All Over The World?

As you have learned by now about us frogs, we are amphibians and we are most diverse and widespread.

We frogs and toads in total do include more than 4800 different species that researchers do know about today. New frog and toad species are also being discovered all of the time.

So, you might wonder where you can find us and where the heck we frogs are hiding. You can basically find us frogs around the world, but you must always open your eyes to the many wonders of nature...

Tyler's tree frog. This frog has large toe pads and webbed feet to be able to walk in the woods

Here are the places where we like hanging around most:
    We frogs are found in
    Africa (South Africa; Madagascar, Tanzania, Switzerland; Zimbabwe)
    Asia (China, Hong Kong, India, Japan, Philippines)
    North America (Canada, United States)

Central and Southern America (Colombia, Costa Rica, Panama Bolivia, Brazil, Ecuador, French Guiana, Guyana, Peru, Belize, Guatemala, Honduras, Mexico, Nicaragua Argentina, Paraguay, Venezuela)

Australia and South Pacific (Papua New Guinea, Solomon Islands, Australia, Indonesia, Fiji), Europe and Middle East (Spain, Greece, Israel, Portugal).

There are approximately 4,740+ species of us frogs without counting the toads around the entire world. There are about 90 species of frogs in the United States.

You can find frogs on every continent in the world except Antarctica. However, you will discover the highest concentration of our species in the waremer and cozier tropical places and cimates.

Besides living on dry land and in fresh water, some species of us adult frogs are adapted for living underground and on trees so make sure to look on the ground and below your feet and high up in the air so that you can discover us frogs because we love to hide on trees and deep in the woods where we have great hiding places underground.

What Is The Body System, Life Cycle & Lifespan Of Frogs?

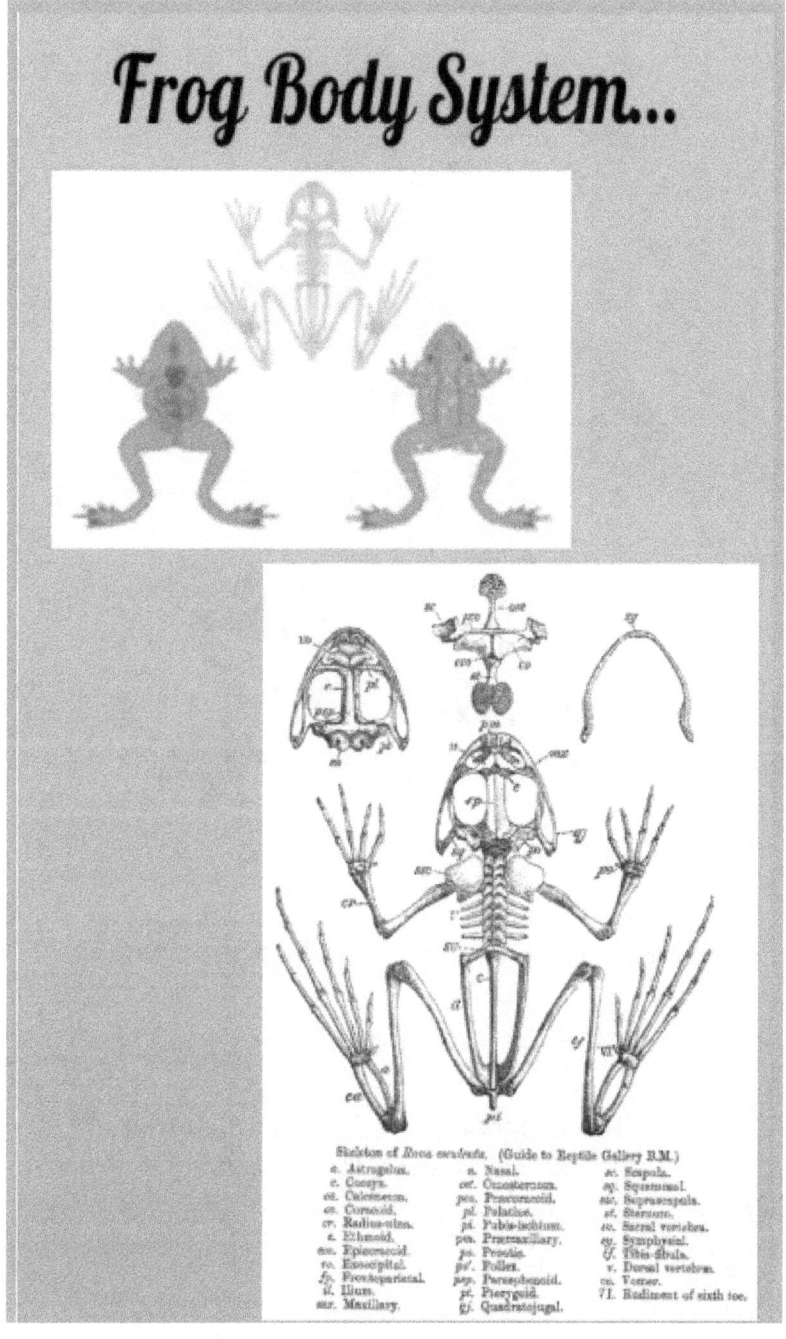

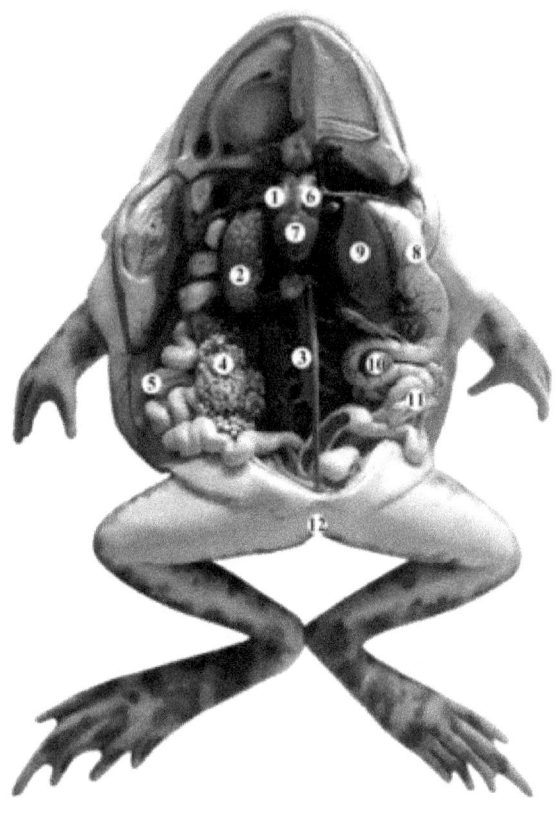

Source: Picture taken by Jonathan McIntosh
Frog anatomy display in NMH Washington DC, US

**Source: Picture taken by Jonathan McIntosh
Frog anatomy display in NMH Washington DC, US**

1. Right atrium
    2. Lungs
    3. Aorta
    4. Egg mass
    5. Colon
    6. Left atrium

7. Ventricle
8. Stomach
9. Liver
10. Gallbladder
11. Small intestine
12. Cloaca

The body plan of us adult frogs is typically characterized by a stout body, a cleft tongue, protruding eyes, limbs that are folded underneath, and the absence of a tail.

We frogs have an endoskeleton. It is made of bone to support our body weight, but we come without a rib cage.

Our skin is moist for respiration.

Our sense organs do include eyes and ears.

We tadpoles do excrete Ammonia through gills and kidneys and pretty much like a fish is doing it.

Our kidneys helps us remove nitrogen waste from our blood circulation and mix it with water to make urine out of it.

Our female counterparts do lay eggs.

Hormones help regulate our body systems (metabolism, heart rate, metamorphosis, and sexual development).

Eyes

Our eyes (and the pairs of eyes of most of us frogs) are located on either side of our heads and very close to the top. Our eyes project outwards as hemispherical bulges.

They provide binocular vision over a field of 100° to the front and a total visual field of almost 360°.

Our eyes may be the only part of an otherwise submerged frog to protrude from the water.

Each eye has closable upper and lower lids and a nictitating membrane which provides us with some further protection, especially when we frogs are swimming.

Yes, we members of the aquatic family of the Pipidae have our eyes located at the top of our head, which is truly a position that is better suited for detecting prey in the water above, too!

The irises of our eyes do come in a ranges of colors and our pupils do come in a range of weird shapes.

The Bufo bufo (a common toad), for example, has beautiful golden irises and horizontal slit like pupils.

The red eyed tree frog, for example, has some vertical slit pupils.

The poison dart frog, another beautiful and colorful looking frog that is part of our frog family, has dark irises.

The fire bellied toad on the other hand comes with some triangular pupils whereas the tomato frog has circular pupils.

The irises of the southern toad, however, come with patterns so as to blend in with the surrounding camouflaged skin.

Adult Southern Toad

Sight & Vision

The distant vision of us frogs is better than our near vision. When we are calling we will quickly become silent when we see an enemy or intruder or a weird moving shadow. However, the closer an object is in relation to our eyes the lesser we are able to see it.

When we frogs do shoot our our tongue to catch flies and insects we are reacting to a small moving object that we can not see well. We must line it up precisely beforehand because we are shutting our eyes as our tongue is extended.

Close-up of a frog's head showing an eye, nostril, mouth and tympanum

Does A Frog See Colors?

The scientists are not sure if we frogs can see in color or not!

Some researchers have made tests with us and found out that we do responds positively to blue light.

They figured that maybe because that same blue color is associated with water that can provide refuge and a hiding place that we like to use when we frogs feels threatened!

Well, I leave the question open for more debate because we frogs certainly do not want to tell all our secrets that have helped us to survive for millions of years.

Maybe, the next time you visit us in the zoo, you can take a closer look at us to get more insight and knowledge about our senses in relation to colors!

Life Cycle Of A Frog

The life cycle of us frogs is finished when we metamorphose into adult frogs and once we are adult frogs we can start the whole process of metamorphose from the beginning and this is how it goes over and over again. You can learn more details about this whole process and learn the individual stages of the metamorphose in the next chapter where we are talking about mating and reproduction of us frogs...

Source: LadyofHats
The diferent stages in the life of the Northern Green Frog

Lifespan Of Frogs and Toads

In captivity, many species of us frogs and toads can live for very long times. The average lifespan is around 4 and 15 years.

The longest lifespan that has ever been recorded was for an European Common Toad with a lifespan of 40 years.

Other frog and toad species which live very long in captivity are the following:

Giant Toad: between seven and twenty-four years.

Ornate Horned Frog: from five to twelve years

Oriental Fire-bellied Toad: between eleven and fourteen years

Green And Black Poison Dart Frog: between seven and seventeen years

How Do Frogs Mate & Reproduce?

Source: Christian Fischer
Male of the Common Midwife Toad, with eggs at its hind legs

The eggs of our female frogs are produced after the result of external fertilisation. Our females release eggs and the sperm from male touches it which results in the development of the egg...

and then...

We male frogs together with the female frogs maintain a posture called amplexus position. We like to keep this position because it helps us with better mating. We frogs can stay in such an amplexus position for hours or even for days as the female releases as few as one or as many as several hundred eggs...

and then...

We frogs typically lay our eggs in water...

...but a few species of us deposit eggs on land or bypass the tadpole stage.

After getting moisture we frogs start developing. A few of us species carry their eggs in their vocal sacs or their abdomens. Others lay eggs in dry areas and keep the eggs moist with water or urine. Depending on the frog's species and the climate in which it typically lives, the eggs can hatch in a few days to a few weeks....

Tadpoles that live in temporary rainwater ponds often become frogs in a couple of weeks. The process that we are calling metamorphosis can take months in species that live in permanent lakes, rivers and ponds and it depends on various other factors.

The Life Cycle Of A Frog

Below you can learn the individual stages that are happening from the aquatic larvae phase to the last phase where the aquatic larvae develops into a juvenile frog with tail. The last part of this cycle is called metarmophosis.

Stage 1
The eggs hatch into aquatic larvae called tadpoles that have tails and internal gills.
They have highly specialized rasping mouth parts suitable for herbivorous, omnivorous or planktivorous diets.

In a few species, fully formed froglets hatch from the eggs, but most of the time the frog starts its life as a tadpole.

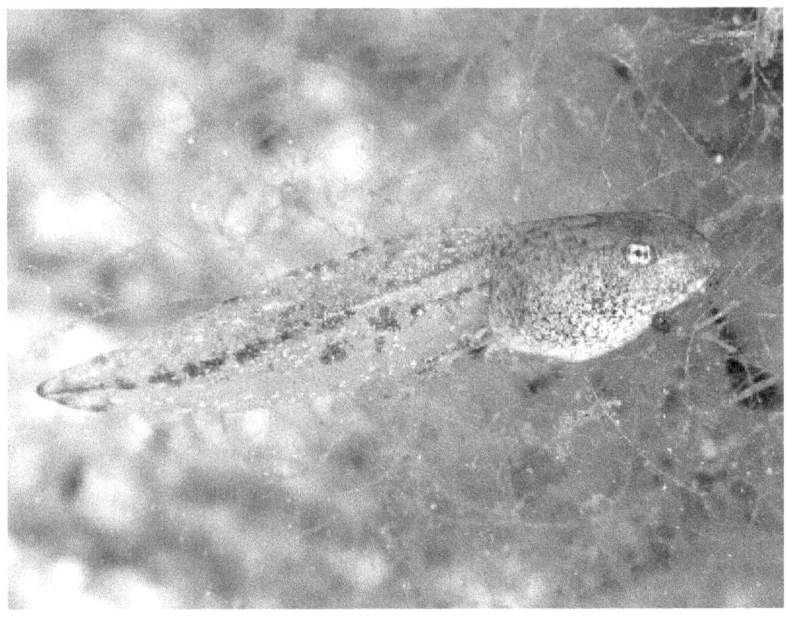

**Source: Viridiflavus Larva of the common frog
Rana temporaria - a day before metamorphosis happens**

Stage 2

Source: Viridiflavus—Metamorphosis stage with deforming jaws, large eyes, and remains of gill pouch

Stage 3

Tadpoles that live in temporary rainwater ponds often become frogs in a couple of weeks. The process can take months in species that live in permanent lakes, rivers and ponds.

Source: Chemicalinterest (talk)—Juvenile frog with tail

The Process Of Metamorphosis

At the end of the tadpole stage, we frogs do undergo a process called metamorphosis in which our body makes a sudden transition into the adult form of a frog.

This metamorphosis typically lasts only 24 hours, and is initiated by production of the hormone thyroxine. This causes different tissues to develop in different ways. The principal changes that take place include the development of the lungs and the disappearance of the gills and gill pouch, making our front legs visible.

Our lower jaw transforms into the big mandible of the carnivorous adult. The long and spiral gut of the herbivorous tadpole is replaced by the typical short gut of a predator.

Our nervous system becomes adapted for hearing and stereoscopic vision, and for new methods of locomotion and feeding.

Our eyes are repositioned higher up on the head and our eyelids and associated glands are formed.

Our eardrum, middle ear, and inner ear are developed. Our skin becomes thicker and tougher, the lateral line system is lost, and our skin glands are developed.

The final stage is the disappearance of the tail, but this takes place rather later, the tissue being used to produce a spurt of growth in our limbs.

We frogs are the most vulnerable to predators when we are undergoing metamorphosis.

At this time, our tail is being lost and locomotion by the means of our limbs is only just becoming established so we are very easy targets for enemies during this vulnerable process of metamorphosis.

Let's look at the next chapter were we frogs show you what we are able to do once we become tough adult frogs.

Yep, we might me delicate and vulnerable as juvenile frogs, but once we are developed into adult frogs, we can be pretty mean and aggressive if someone attacks us...

Did you know that one of our species can even kill human predators that attack him with his poisonous and toxic secretion that the frog will ooze via its skin?

Not all of us are poisonous, but some of us are and you are going to discover the reason why in the next chapter where you will discover all the secrets of our slimy and colorful skin.

You will also learn about the most poisonous species of us frogs in the upcoming chapters. I will show you the most poisonous frogs on earth, the most bizarre looking frogs on earth, and the most handsome frogs on earth so that you are aware of the differences.

Why Do Frogs Have Moist Skin & Why Do They Shed Their Skin?

Our skin is semi-permeable which is making us susceptible to dehydration, so we either live in moist places or we have special adaptations to deal with dry habitats.

Moist Skin

We frogs have moist skin which protects us and it also has a respiratory function for us.

Our skin also absorbs water and helps us control our body temperature.

We frogs have many glands, particularly on our head and our back, which help us release poisonous and distasteful substances. These secretions are often sticky and the substance does protect us against the entry of bacteria and mould.

Theses substances make us look slimy and slippery and like this we are capable to escape from dangerous predators.

...Aren't we slimy looking?

Skin Shedding

We are part of the amphibian family like the salamanders and we frogs therefore moult regularly.

We frogs are moulting regularly and we do consume our skin, too!

Some of us frog species are moulting in pieces and others in one single piece.

The process of moulting or molting can be described as this. Amphibians like frogs and salamanders are shedding and sloughing. For other species this process is also called ecdysis which is the manner in which an animal routinely is casting off part of the body (often but not always this process is an outer layer or covering process and it depends on the specific amphibian species).

Shedding and molting happens at a very specific time of the year, but it might also happen at a very specific point in the life cycle/life stages of an amphibian.

Moulting can, for example, involve the shedding of our skin, hair, feathers, fur, and wool, or it might involve the external layer. In some species of amphibians, other body parts may be shed, too. For example, in some insects, their wings or the entire exoskeleton in arthropods.

This shedding aspect alone is a very curious and interesting aspect of our species! Don't you think?

Source: Mokele—A Rana pipiens moulting and eating the skin

Beautiful Skin Colors

The color of us frog's skin is used for thermo-regulation. In cool damp conditions our color will be darker than on a hot dry day. Aren't we some fascinating creatures?

The Red-eyed Tree Frog

Toxic & Poisonous Secretions

As I already told you before the skin of us frogs is glandular, with secretions ranging from distasteful to toxic and weird secretions and below you will find some cool pictures that demonstrates this poisonous aspect of our frog skin...

Blue Poison Dart frog at Bristol Zoo,
Bristol, England

Source: Deepinon

Toad Warts

The more warty looking species the Anura orger (frogs) is called toads.

The bumps on a toad's skin is actually very useful for the toad because it helps it blend into the nature in a visual way.

Frog or toad warts are elevations in the skin where glandular toxins tend to concentrate.

The distinction between frogs and toads is based on informal naming conventions concentrating on the warts rather than evolutionary history and heritage. Some toads are more closely related to us frogs than other toads are....

Source: Bill Lionheart

Camouflage

Our skin varies in colors from well-camouflaged dappled browns, greys and greens to more vivid patterns of bright reds or yellows and blacks to advertise our toxicity and warn off predators...

Source: Sztraka38

...Do you see me with my camouflage hiding mask on?

Oxygen & Skin

Many of us frogs are able to absorb oxygen directly through our skin....

Some of us absorb oxygen through our skin, and for this to happen in a proper manner, our skin must be moist.

A disadvantage of our moist skin is however that pathogens can thrive on it which is increasing the chance of infections.

To not let that happen we frogs secrete peptides that destroy these pathogens. I told you that we are pretty smart creatures! Didn't I?

Yes we use our ancient wisdom and secrets to survive on earth and not let predators take us!

Source: Leonora Enking from West Sussex, England —The Green Tree Frog in Australia, White's Tree Frog, or Dumpy Tree Frog is a species of tree frog native to Australia and New Guinea, with introduced populations in New Zealand and the US.

Do Frogs Use A Defence Mechanisms?

We frogs must always be on the lookout because many dangers lure around. Humans and other predators might want to eat us.

This is why we frogs hide under stones and leaves (this is also an example for applying camouflage like you have seen in the last chapter).

Camouflage is a common defensive mechanism that we frogs are using to hide from predators. We find out a position where we can blend into the background and remain undetected. Some of us frogs have the ability to change our color, but this is usually restricted to only a small range of colors.

For example, one of our species, the White's tree frog, varies between pale green colors and dull brown colors according to the temperature and climate.

Another defence mechanism of ours is staying very still without moving. The Gray Tree Frog, another one of our species, likes to practice this method as a way to stay alive. The predators of this frog think that the Gray Tree Frog is dead and they will not mess around with it.

In some of us frogs, our skin glands help us secrete foul tasting chemicals and this poisons are uses by us for protection.

Source: Lukasz Olszewski ImreKiss
A common toad adopting a defensive position

When you look at us frogs, you might notice that at first we seem rather defenceless.

Why?

You got it! It is our small size, our slow movement, our skin, and our lack of defensive structures like our claws, teeth, and spine that makes us look weak and defenseless.

Many of us use tactics like camouflage (spotted skin, streaked skin in neutral colors). Camouflage allows us stationary frogs to merge into our environement and surroundings.

Some of us can make prodigious leaps that often takes them into the water in order to evade potential attacks.

Other frog species do have even creepier defensive adaptations and strategies.

These frogs, for example, use their skin for defense like discusses in the previous chapter.

The skin of many of our frog species contains mild toxic substances.

The glands that can be found on toads and some of us frogs produce secrete mucus and a range of toxins. These secretions make toads and us frogs look slippery so that no one even thinks about grabbing and groping us!

Who would like to touch a slimey, distasteful, and poisonous creature?

I hope you are liking our weird defense secrets!

If the noxious effects that we are transporing via our skin is immediate, the predator who tries to attack us may stop the actions so that we can escape.

If the noxious effect develops in a slower way, the predator may even learn to avoid our species in future. This is what we frogs call true intelligence because we were actually able to teach our predators not to attack and harm us!

The poisonous frogs among us tend to promote their toxicity with very bright and shiny colors. This is an adaptive defense strategy that is known as aposematism.

The poison dart frog, for example, are using such a defense mechanism that applies the art of aposematism.

Our relatives, the poison dart frogs, are typically in bright reds, oranges, or yellows, and often with contrasting black colored markings on their skin.

Did you know that the native people of South America even extract poison from these poison dart frogs to apply to their own self defense and their weapons for hunting?

At least two non poisonous species of us frogs in the tropical forests of America like to mimic the coloration of the dart poison frogs for self protection and self defense purposes.

Strawberry poison-dart frog contains numerous alkaloids which deter predators

We frogs also like to deceive our predators with a defense mechanism that we call mimicking the appearance of two different toxic species with which we share a common range.

Other species of us frog, such as the European fire bellied toad, show their warning color underneath and this is how they defend themselves.

They "flash" when being attacked and they even adopt a pose that exposes the vivid and bright coloring on their bellies to shock the predator.

Some other frogs even obtain poison from ants and other arthropods that they eat!

Others, such as our relatives, the Australian corroboree frogs, can synthesize these poisonous alkaloids themselves in order to defend themselves.

The chemicals involve some wicked poisons like nerve poisons and other weird types of poisons.

Many predators of us frogs have become adapted to tolerate even the highest levels of our poisons, but other predators, including the human being, who like to attack us frogs, may be severely affected by our poisonous defense system.

Some of us frogs use bluff and even deception tricks for defense.

The European common toad, for example, adopts a characteristic stance when being attacked. The European common toad is inflating the body and standing with its hindquarters raised and with a lowered head position.

The bullfrog is able to crouche down with the eyes closed and the head tipped forward when it is threatened. This is a position that helps the bullfrog to place the parotoid glands in the most effective position. The other glands on the bullfrog's back begin to ooze poisonous and noxious secretions in an effort to protect its most vulnerable parts of the body. If the bullfrog is touched on the back, the predator will feel this poisonous effect and hopefully will leave the bullfrog alone.

Another secret tactic that we frogs use for our defense is sound.

Some of us frogs "scream" out and this sudden loud noise interrupts the predator and it tends to startle the attacker.

The gray tree frog, for example, makes an explosive sound. This sound repels the shrew Blarina brevicauda. This is a shrew predator in the genus Blarina and it often occurs in the northeastern region of North America and it is one of our many predators that we like to scare off with our weird sound

defense mechanism!

The defense strategy employed by juvenile American toads on being approached and eaten by a snakes is to crouch down and remain in an immobile position. This tactic is usually successful, with the snakes passing by and the toad remaining undetected in this position. If the toad is encountered by the snake, the toad quickly hops away before crouching defensively.

These are just some of our most secretly guarded defense tricks and tactics and we do apply many more. I also remind you of the fact that there are thousands of frog species on earth and every frog has a slightly different way of doing it.

I can not list all of the different defense tricks of all our frog species in this book because you would never be able to finish the book.

I told you that we frogs are creepy, weird, and curious, and intriguing critters and in this frog defense chapter you finally found the proof!

What Are Various Sizes & Colors Of Frogs?

Source: Patrick Gijsbers—The bright colors of this granular poison frog serve as a warning to predators of its noxious taste.

The Warning Colorations Of Us Frogs Are Useful For Our Defense & Beautiful To Look At, too!

Toads and we frogs vary greatly in size. Members of the tree frog family, for example, some less than 1 inch long are more frequently heard than seen. The true frog family includes the largest frog in Minnesota, the bullfrog, which may measure up to 8 inches in length.

In general, adult female toads and frogs are larger than males of the same species. Isn't that totally weird and backwards?

Yes, we frogs do consist of some very diverse and colorfull species. During our breeding season, the male toads and we make frogs have a darker throat color than our female counterparts and male toads grow pads on their thumbs, too!

Some of us frogs can even adjust the color according to the changes in the light, the moisture, the temperature, or even our mood that we are in!

Oh, there are psychic frogs, you might exclaim! I remind you of the fact that we frogs are some weird creatures. Didn't I tell you?

Be surprised for some more creepy features and behaviors that I will help you discover throughout the next chapters. In the chapter the most bizarre looking freaks you are in for a real treat!

Whites Tree Frogs, for example, are usually light green coloured. When tree frogs do move out of a sunny spot into a damp, or shady spot, however, their color sometimes changes to a lighter brown color.

There is even one type of us frogs that survives in the desert just by changing its colors from a brown and dark color to a bright white color during the bright and sunny hours of the day. The white would reflect the sun so that this frog can keep from getting dried up and die in the heat.

Do All Frogs Sound The Same?

The answer is no! Not all of us frogs sound the same because not every frog does make a similar sound. Different species of us frogs make many different kinds of sounds. The most known frog sound is the croaking sound that some people call ribbit. Some other people call it kwaaks.

We frogs produce a wide range of vocalizations, particularly in their breeding season, and exhibit many different kinds of complex behaviors to attract mates, to fend off predators, and to generally survive.

Every different species of frog makes its own special sound and it is only the male frog that can croak. They have a small sac in their throats that vibrates the air as they slowly let it out.

The sounds that we frogs make are not what you'd expect neither!

Did you know that we frogs do chirp? Others can whistle, croak, ribbit, peep, cluck, bark, and grunt.

The call or croak of us frogs is unique to our species. We frogs create our sounds by passing air through the larynx in the throat. In most of our frog callings, our sound is amplified by one or more of our vocal sacs. These are the membranes of our skin and under our throat or on the corner of our mouth.

Our membrane distends during the amplification of our call. Some frog calls are so loud that they can be heard up to a mile away.

There are other frogs (genera Heleioporus and Neobatrachus) that lack vocal sacs entirely, but these frogs still can produce a loud call. The buccal cavity of these frogs is enlarged and dome-shaped, acting as a resonance chamber that amplifies their sounds. Other species of us frogs that lack vocal sacs and that do not have a loud call tend to inhabit areas that are close to a constant noise, flowing water, etc. These frogs need to use an alternative means to communicate. The coastal tailed frog (Ascaphus truei) lives in mountain streams in North America and this frog species does not vocalize at all.

You must be aware of the reasons why we frogs are making these sounds.

Well, the main reason for our calling is to allow us male frogs to attract female mates. We male frogs may call individually or there may be a chorus of sound where numerous of us male frogs have converged on breeding sites.

Females of many frog species, such as the common tree frog, reply to our male calls. This male mating calling acts to reinforce reproductive activity in a breeding colony of frogs.

Our female frogs prefer males that produce sounds of greater intensity and lower frequency, which are attributes that stand out in a crowd. The rationale for our calling behavior is thought to be that by demonstrating such a powerful sound to the female frogs, we males demonstrate that we are superior and able to produce superior offspring.

A different frog call is emitted by us male frogs or unreceptive female frogs during the mating process. This is a distinct chirruping sound and is accompanied by a vibration of our body.

Tree frogs and some non-aquatic species have a rain call that they make on the basis of humidity cues prior to a shower.

Many species of us frogs also have a territorial call that is used to drive away other males. All of these calls are emitted with our mouth closed.

A distress call that is emitted by some of us frogs when we are in danger is produced with our mouth open. This is resulting in a higher pitched call. This type of call is typically used by us when we are being groped and grabbed by a predator.

This sound serves us in distracting and disorientating the predator attacker so the enemy releases us immediately because of the loud and shocking sound that they did not anticipate.

Many species of us frogs have deep calls. The croak of the American bullfrog, for exaple, is sometimes written as "jug o' rum".

The Pacific tree frog, another species of us frogs, does produce the onomatopoeic "ribbit" that you can often heard in films.

Humans try to imitate our callings with words like: "brekekekex koax koax" and other weird words that really have nothing in common with our true frog sounds.

You can see by now that we frogs are a pretty unique and complicated creature and we all have different behaviors when it comes to making sounds.

I hope that by now you have already a better idea about us frogs. Hopefully you appreciate our existence because appreciation and respect for us creatures is what ultimately is going to open your eyes to get even deeper into the discovery phase. Once you are changing your perspective and look at the world from our perspective, you will exactly know who we are!

Frog Movements: Hibernation & Locomotion

Source: Brian Gratwicke—Rainforest Rocket Frog Jumping (jumping is part of a frog's locomotion)

Torpor or Hibernation

Hibernation is a state of decreased physiological activity. We frogs can usually operate and survive on a reduced rate of metabolism and body temperature.

Hibernation is used to enable us frogs to survive periods of reduced food availability in the winter time.

What happens during hibernation?

During the most extreme conditions and in order to survive we frogs do enter a state of hibernation and during this phase we remain inactive for months.

In colder regions of the earth, many species of us frogs do hibernate during the winter time.

Those that live on the dry land such as the American toad are digging a burrow and make a hibernaculum for themselves in which they are staying in a dormant position.

Source: Cephas—Eastern American Toad

Other toads that are less proficient at digging a hibernaculum are able to find a crevice or they do burry themselves under some dead leaves on the ground. Aquatic frog species such as the American bullfrog sink to the bottom of a pond where they are semi-immersed under mud. These frogs are still able to access the oxygen that is dissolved in the water.

Our metabolism slows down and we live on our energy reserves. Some of us frogs can even survive being totally frozen. Can you imagine a frozen frog (all tissues and blood is frozen) that is still able to survive!

Ice crystals form under our skin and our body cavity are our most essential organs and they are protected from freezing by a high concentration of glucose.

If you discover us in an apparently lifeless and frozen state, be asured that we frogs can resume respiration and our heart beat can restart again when conditions are warm enough like in the spring.

Locomotion

We frogs love to be very active when it is not cold and therefore all the different species of us frogs are exercising a number of movements that are most adequate for us: running, walking, jumping, swimming, climbing, burrowing, and gliding.

Jumping

Yes, we froggies are usually recognized by folks for our exceptional jumping skills!

This is a true skill or ours and our jumping skills are relative to our size. We frogs are the best jumpers of all vertebrates.

The Australian rocket frog, one of our buddies, for example, can leap over 2 metres (6 feet and 7 inches). This is a distance that is more than 50 times the body length of the Australian rocket frog. The body size is only 5.5 centimetres (2.2 inches).

There are tremendous differences between us frog species in our jumping capabilities. Within a species, our jump distance increases in relation increased size. The Indian skipper frog, for example, has the ability to leap out of the water from a position floating on the surface.

The tiny northern cricket frog that you can see below can "skitter" across the surface of a pond with a series of short rapid jumps.

Source: Patrick Coin—Northern Cricket Frog

Walking And Running

Our pals the frogs in the families of Bufonidae have very short back legs and they also tend to walk rather than jump.

When these frogs are trying to move rapidly, they speed up the rate of their moves. They can speed up the movement of their limbs or they can even resort to an ungainly hopping gait which is truly amazing to watch!

The western narrow-mouthed toad has been described as having a gait that is a combination of short hops and leaps and running. These funny moves are usually only an inch or two in length.

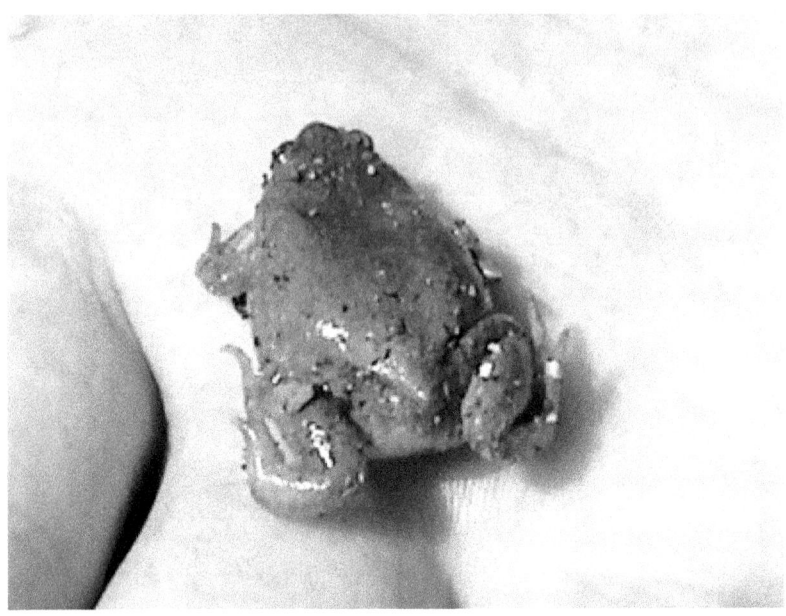

Source: Dawson—western narrow-mouthed toad

In an experiment, one of our buddie's the Fowler's toad was placed on a treadmill which was turned at varying speeds. By measuring the toad's uptake of oxygen it was found that hopping was an inefficient use of resources during sustained locomotion but was a useful strategy during short bursts of high-intensity activity.

Source: Jimpaz—A Fowler's Toad displaying its camouflage in the leaves
The red-legged running frog has short, slim hind limbs unsuited to jumping. It can move fast by using a running gait in which the two hind legs are used alternately. Slow motion photography shows that, unlike a horse that can trot or gallop, the frog's gait remained similar at slow, medium and fast speeds.

Source: Dawson—Red Legged Running Frog

This species can also climb trees, and shrubs and does so at night to catch insects.

The Indian skipper frog has broad feet and can run across the surface of the water for several metres (yards).

Source: Saleem Hameed—Indian skipper frog

Swimming

Many of us frogs that live in ponds, damps, rivers, or that visit water regularly have adaptations that improve their swimming skills. The hind limbs of us frogs are strong because we are muscled. The webbing between ours toes of the hind feet increases the area of our feet and helps us propel in a powerful way through the water.

Members of us frogs who are totally aquatic do show the most marked specialization for swimming. We frogs have a very inflexible vertebral column, a flattened and streamlined body, a lateral line system, and a powerful hind limbs with large webbed feet.

Tadpoles are well equipped for swimming, too because they have large tail-fins which provide thrust when they move their tail from one side to the other.

Burrowing

Some of our buddies have become true adapters and they adapted their body and life around the art of burrowing and a life underground. These species tend to have short limbs, rounded and bloated bodies, small heads with bulging eyes. They use their hind feet that are adapted for excavation. An extreme example of such adaption for burrowing is the Purple frog from southern India. It feeds on termites and spends almost its whole life living underground.

The purple frog only emerges briefly during the monsoon months to mate and breed in temporary pools. It has a tiny little head with a pointed snout and a plump rounded and bloated body that is perfectly adapted for burrowing.

The purple frog is one of our frog species that truly loves burrowing.

The spadefoot toads of North America are also adapted to a life underground. The plains spadefoot toad has a flap of keratinised bone attached to one of its metatarsals of its hind foot which it uses to dig itself backwards into the ground.

Source: Takwish—Spadefoot Toad

As this weird creature keeps digging, it wriggles its hips from side to side in order to sink into the loose soil.

This toad is also known to emerge in the middle of the night in order to forage (looking for food).

In winter times, the toad is digging much deeper.

The tunnel dug by the toad is filled with soil and the toad hibernates in a small chamber at the end of it.

The process of hibernation helps the toad to stay alive.

Spadefoot toads are "explosive breeders", as well! These toads are emerging from their burrows at the same time and converging on temporary pools. They are attracted by the calling of the first toad male to find a suitable breeding location.

In Australia we burrowing frogs do lead a rather different lifestyle.

The western spotted frog, for example, digs a burrow in the bed of an ephemeral stream or next to a river. The frog emerges on a regular basis from its burrow to look for food (forage).

As soon as the mating phase begins, the frogs place their eggs and the eggs are laid in a foam nest inside the burrow. The eggs partially develop inside the burrow and they do not hatch out until they are submerged following very heavy rainfalls.

The tadpoles then are forced to swim out into the open water and environment and they are able to rapidly complete their development into juvenile frogs.

Our Madagascan burrowing frog pals, on the other side, are less fossorial and bury themselves under leaf litter that lays on the ground.

The green burrowing frog, for example, has a flattened head with a short snout and well developed metatarsal tubercles on its hind feet to help with excavation.

It also has greatly enlarged terminal discs on its fore feet that help it to clamber around in bushes.

It breeds in temporary pools that form after rains.

Climbing

Our pal the tree frog is found high in the canopy where he scrambles around on the tree branches, twigs and the leaves.

Sometimes the tree frog never comes down to earth.

Source: Christoph Leeb—Tree Frog

Most tree frogs are under 10 cm (4 inches) in length. They have long legs and long toes with sticky pads on the tips which helps them with climbing onn trees.

Their sticky toe pads provides them with the best grip on any wet or dry surface, including slippery surfaces and glass.

Tree frogs are very acrobatic and sportive because they are able to catch insects while they are simultaneously hanging with one toe from a twig or clutching onto the blade of a windswept reed.

Some other frogs that are closely related to the tree frog have opposable toes on their feet. The reticulate leaf frog for example has a single opposed digit on each fore foot and this frog also has two opposed digits on the hind feet.

This anatomy and body features/functions allow this frog to grasp the stem of a bushe as it clambers around in its riverside environment and habitat.

Gliding

During the evolutionary history of my frog pals, several different groups of frogs have independently taken to the air.

Some of my frog friends in the tropical rainforest are specially adapted for gliding from one tree to another tree or parachuting from the top of a tree to the tropical forest floor.

One of my buddies, the Wallace flying frog from Malaysia and Borneo is a funny gliding frog. Overall, it looks much like the green flying frog.

The Wallace flying frog has large feet and they expand with the fingertips into one flat sticky disc.

There are flaps of skin on the lateral margins of the frog's limbs and across the tail region, too.

With the sticky digits splayed, the limbs outstretched and the flaps spread, the Wallace flying frog can glide a considerable distance.

The Wallace flying frog is unable to undertake a powered flight.

It can also alter its direction of travel and it is able to navigate a long distance of up to 15 metres (49 feet) between trees.

Where Do Frogs Go In The Winter & Hibernation

We frogs do receive heat from our external environment. During the winter time, the low temperatures make it very difficult to be active as a frog. So the strategy that we are following during the winter time is to hibernate and live off of stored body fat. We frogs do not required heat energy due to our reduced rate of our metabolism.

The fat that is stored in our bodies helps us store energy that we need during the time of hibernation.

Some of our species jump into the water and prepare to hibernate at the bottom of ponds or under the banks of streams becaise water is a good insulator and retains the heat better than other environments do. We frogs love to hybernate at places like the bottom of a pond or similar places until the winter goes away.

Once the winter time is over we can get into our active phase and mating again until the next winter comes and we get into the hibernation phase again. During our hibernation phase we are changing our positions and behaviors.

When spring arrives and when we come out of hibernation we are opening our eyes and we are aware of all the things that are happening in our environment around us.

Spring time is the time where we are most active and we are hanging around in trees, woods, ponds, and other fun and natural places that provide the perfect climate and temperature for us so that we can jump around and do what we do best: croaking, whistling, ribbiting, peeping, clucking, barking, and grunting...

How Does A Frog Obtain Its Food?

We frogs do eat various types of insects like flies, mosquitoes and other harmful insects. If you are plagued by flies and want to get rid of them, let us know because we can help.

We also like to eat snails, spiders, fish, worms, and here is the kicker: even other frogs!

How do we frogs eat our food? We have a long and sticky tongue that flicks in and out and this is how we are catching our food.

Even though we have tiny teeth on our upper jaw and on the roof of our mouth.

We are able to hold prey with these teeth. We frogs pull our eyes down into the roof of our mouth which helps us push the food down our throat.

We adult frogs are carnivores and larvae are herbivores. Once a juvenile frog enters adulthood, the frog changes his eating habits from eating herbs into eating meat.

We adult frogs usually have a carnivorous diet that consists of small invertebrates, but there are frogs that are on a omnivorous diet. These frogs are considered to be the omnivorous species (these frogs eat herbs and meat).

A few frog species only feed on fruits.

By the way did you know that we frogs are extremely efficient at converting what we are eating into body mass, which makes us an extremely important food source for predators and that is probably the reason why we have learned to defend ourselves in such an effective way!

If you have not read about our sneaky defense system in the previous chapter, make sure to take a look at how we frogs are true ninjas at self defense.

Which Are The Most Poisonous Frogs On Earth?

In this chapter I will show you the most poisonous and venemous frog creatures of the planet so make sure to take good note on these xx species of frogs because not every frog might turn into a prince. There are frogs that are poisonous and dangerous so you must make sure that you know the differences between poisonous frogs and frogs that do not cause any harm.

Never try to touch or come close to a frog if you do not know what frog or creature you are dealing with.

This book helps you to identify the most poisonous and dangerous frogs, the most bizarre looking frogs that are just weird looking but not dangerous, and the most handsome and friendly frogs that do not harm you.

Golden Poison Dart Frog

Let's get started with the first poisonous frog that features a bright colored skin in yellow color and that lives in Central and South America. Make a note of the following. When these species is in danger, they send out a visual warning to predators: "Do Not Eat Me!"

You have to know that many frogs of this family ooze out a deadly poison. This happens through their poisonous skin and this is how these creatures are protecting themselves against predators. This is their defence mechanism.

Their size varies from around ¾ to 2 ¾ inches in size. They love to eat insects, termites, and ants. They do live in various habitats, but they prefer the more tropical regions where they can keep a most skin.

This species of frog lays a small number of eggs and they do provide some parental care for the juvenile frogs.

Source: Marcel Burkhard

The golden poison frog is one of the most poisonous creatures on earth. It originates from Central and South America. This creature is so dangerous because it contains enough poison to kill 20,000 mice or even 10 people. It is so poisonous that even touching it can be a dangerous adventure.

Never touch a frog that you do not know!

The golden poison frog is 2 inches in size and it is found mostly in Western Colombia. Its habitat is on the ground in lowland rain forest or often near the rivers. The golden poison frog is found in moist tropical rain forests. These dangerous frogs also lay eggs on land. When their tadpoles hatch, the male carries them on his back to a larger area of water, where they will complete their metamorphosis.

The golden poison dart frog is considered one of the most toxic animals on Earth. A single specimen measuring two inches (five centimetres) has enough venom to kill ten grown men.

These brightly coloured amphibians are among the largest of the more than 100 poison dart frog species, averaging more than one inch (two and a half centimetres) in length. They live within a tiny plot of rain forest on the Pacific coast of Colombia. And though the population in its small range is abundant, but due to lack of rainfall, it is becoming endangered.

They can be found in colours of yellow, orange, or pale green, depending on their particular range. Their diet includes flies, crickets, ants, termites, and beetles.

Dendrobates Azureus

Source: Quartl

Source: Wildfeuer

The Dendrobates azureus or otherwise known as Blue Poison Frogs are poison dart frogs.

They can easily be identified because of its bright blue color with small black spots that are all over their entire skin. These dark spots are slightly bigger in the middle of this frog's back.

Blue Poison Frogs come in a bright blue color. The bright blue color is like a warning system to other predators to not eat them.

The bright blue color is like a warning system to other predators to not eat them.

This frog is one of our larger species and can measure up to 4 to 5 centimetres. They often are found in the rain forests. They can also be seen along river banks where they love to hide between rocks.

The Dendrobates azureus frog likes it cozy and warm. He loves a moist environment to keep his skin hydrated. The male frog of this species takes care of the eggs and deposits them between some dead leaves. After the eggs are hatched, he carries the tadpoles 1 or 2 at a time to small puddles in tree cavities or water-filled sepals of some plants.

Poison dart frogs are known for their skin toxins. Natives even hunt them down to get this poison for the tips of their arrows.

These frogs are famous for their toxicity.

All the poison dart frogs do contain some level of toxicity. In captivity, however, these frogs lose their toxicity as a result of an altered diet and a change of circumstances.

They live on rainforest floors. They have poison on their skin and touching them might lead to fatal effects for the enemy.

Giant Leaf Frog

These types of frog species inhabit drier parts of the treetops where they prevent themselves from drying out by wiping wax that is produced by special skin glands over their bodies. They are sometimes called waxy frogs. They are laying their eggs on large leaves overhanging the water. As the eggs hatch, the tadpoles fall into the water to begin their development.

This frog's diet includes insects. Their size ranges from 4-5 inches. Giant leaf frogs occupy a large place within the Amazon rain forest.

The skin secretion of this frog contains deltorphin, deltorphin I, deltorphin II and dermorphin.

Dyeing Dart Frog

This is a large poison dart frog and it is a species of poison dart frogs. It is of around 40 to 50 mm with some females reaching 60 mm. It is a bright blue frog with two broad yellow stripes on its back. These stripes are connected by cross bands to form two or three oval blue islands down the back. Their arms and legs are black or deep blue with many bright yellow or black spots. It has a typical erect posture and a distinct tympanum about half the diameter of the eye.

Male frogs can be distinguished from females as they have larger finger discs that cut straight across the tips. Also, only males produce sounds.

The dyeing dart frog is a mildly toxic species of poison dart frog. It produces pumiliotoxins which the frog uses for self defense and survival.

As it is such a variable species, different color morphs of tinctorius have varying degrees of toxicity, too!

Local tribes use the poison of this frog for decoration. Feathers are plucked from young parrots and these frogs are rubbed on the parrots' exposed skin. When the feathers regrow on the parrot, the frog's toxin causes them to appear in yellow and red color rather than green color.

These yellow feathers are very rare and expensive!

Source: Bobo11

Red-backed Poison Frog

The cutie known as the red-backed poison dart frog can be found in the lowland tropical rainforests of Peru and Ecuador. Like all poison dart frogs, these beauties are vividly coloured and patterned, which shows their poison.

Red-backed poison dart frogs have black legs with cobalt or sky-blue pattern, a black belly, and a back that ranges in colour from fiery orange to scarlet in colour, hence the name "red-backed." They usually remain on the ground and can also climb tree trunks. This frog is often sighted.

Also, it is illegal to export these beautiful frogs from their homes in Peru and Ecuador, which helps in keeping this species safe from the pet trade.

Strawberry Poison Dart Frog

This pal called the strawberry poison dart frog is a small frog, only one inch in length with a plump body and thin limbs. It resides in rainforests. Its head and body are of strawberry-red or orange-red color with blue or black lower parts. The bright colours show that the animal is toxic.

The strawberry poison dart frog does not produce his poison. It takes the toxins from animals like mites, ants, beetles, and others

It absorbs the different insects' poisons into its body. The body itself is immune to these toxins. These poisons are stored in the frog's skin glands and just beneath the epidermis.

This defense is especially effective against mammalian and avian attackers and predators. Reptiles and Amazonian ground snakes have a limited resistance to this frog's poison and the frog has to look out for these snakes because attacks happen occasionally.

This frog is found mostly in Central America and Puerto Rico, the frog prefers lowland rain forests.

Males are territorial and when provoked will jump on top of an interloping male, wrestling for up to 20 minutes. While wrestling, both frogs stand on their hind legs and try to push one another to the ground with their front legs. Once one is pinned, the victor, usually the inhabitant of the territory, allows the other to leave.

Strawberry poison dart frogs mate any time of the year, the female laying up to five eggs. After about a week, the eggs hatch and the mother deposits one tadpole per plant. She returns to each tadpole almost every day and lays up to five unfertilized eggs for it to eat.

Lovely Poison Frog

The lovely poison dart frog is a very small frog measuring 2.5 centimetres in length, though females may be slightly larger than males.

The body and flanks of the frog are typically chocolate brown with two yellow or white dorsal stripes.

The limbs are off-white and flecked with brown, and the belly is normally black with a thin reticulum of yellow.

It is also a unique poison dart frog in that there is no real variation between populations. All poison dart frogs are poisonous in nature.

Minor differences in pattern exist between individuals, but no distinct color differences have been discovered until today.

Source: Maciej Pabijan

Golfoduclean frog

This frog is commonly found in the lowlands like the region of Costa Rica. It is common and can be regularly recorded.

What you should know about this frog is that its population is decreasing day by day.

It is a terrestrial frog that prefers living in moist lowlands and wet forests. It lays its eggs on leaves above the ground. Then it carries hatching eggs to small pools for their development.

It is facing threats like being harmed and killed due to human beings and because of mining and water pollution.

Splash-backed Poison Frog

The vivid red or orange skin of the splash-backed poison frog is a danger signal to potential predators. The frog lives in leaf litter on the rain forest floor of the southern Amazon River Basin in South America.

The Splash backed poison frog is also a species of the poison dart frog and is therefore toxic.

Logging, fires, and the illegal pet trade all threaten this frog's population.

Overall, anywhere from 9 to 122 amphibian species have gone extinct since 1980.

Source: Rolf Kolasch

Phantasmal Poison Frog

This frog has a length of approximately 22.6 mm. Its skin is smooth all over the body. The nostril is closer to the snout than its eye. The second finger is shorter than the first. Toes are basally webbed.

The ground color is usually dark red to brown. Three yellow-white stripes are present on the dorsum.

Hind limbs have bright red spots. Individual frogs can be identified by their stripe patterns which are diverse.

It is a species of the poison dart frog. They also have a very radiant skin color and carry powerful poison on their skin.

These frogs are known to carry the strongest toxins and their toxins are known to be lethal.

The Phantasmal poison frog is able to live up to ten years in captivity and this is yet another endangered frog species. Today there are only seven known locations to man in the wild where these creatures are still living.

Source: H. Krisp

Kokoe Poison Dart Frog

It is an average-sized poison dart frog. Male frogs of this species reach 3 centimetres in length. Females are slightly larger and may reach up to 3.2 centimetres long. Females are bulkier and more robust than males as they will fight for mates just as the males will.

The Kokoe poison dart frog is brilliantly coloured and patterned. Always predominantly black, it has two yellow or green dorsal stripes running from the tip of its nose. The black or dark brown legs are peppered with white dots, and the underside is black.

The Kokoe poison dart frog is an intelligent animal. It can distinguish between humans, and it is capable of remembering locations that suit it well weeks after visiting them.

Like most poison dart frogs, it lives in small groups of four to seven with an average of five and it is toxic.

The Kokoe poison frog is the third most poisonous of the poison dart frogs and secretes batrachotoxins through its permeable skin.

In humans, the poison causes a variety of symptom.

This includes pains, fevers, and seizures.

Later, paralysis occurs, too!

While not as toxic as its other relatives that are larger, the black legged dart frog and the golden poison frog, the Kokoe poison frog is still extremely toxic and poisonous.

Source: TomR (Thomas Ruedas)

Black-legged Dart Frog

Source: Esteban Alzate—2 black-legged dart frogs

These frogs are usually colored similarly to golden poison dart frogs.

Their primary color ranges from earthy oranges to pure yellows.

The limbs and belly are flecked with black. This is one of the best ways to differentiate the two species, as the golden poison dart frog lacks these black flecks.

Along with the golden poison dart frog, the black-legged poison dart frog is more arboreal. As a result, it possesses sucker like discs on its toes in order to aid it in climbing of tree trunks and leaves.

It has an adhesive grip. Both males and females have oval-shaped toe discs.

The black-legged poison dart frog is also an intelligent frog. It can distinguish between humans, and it is capable of remembering locations that suits it well weeks after visiting them. It lives in small groups of four to seven with an average of four frogs.

For breeding, groups of black-legged poison dart frogs gather. Males are vocal and will call to females with a pleasing trill. If the female frog is sufficiently impressed, she will allow the male to lead her to a suitable place for egg deposition. Fertilization is external. The clutch size ranges from five to twelve eggs.

Just 150 micrograms of this poison from this animal is enough to kill an adult human being.

Locals often use the poison of this frog for hunting darts.

The poison causes death by respiratory and muscular paralysis.

As with all dart frogs, captive-raised individuals of this frog species are non toxic.

The animals require chemicals that are only found in the wild. These food sources are mainly insects.

In captivity, these chemicals are not available to the Black legged dart frogs because they are feed other food sources without the chemicals.

Source: TomR (Thomas Ruedas)—poisonous black-legged dart frog

Corroboree Frog

Corroboree frogs are among Australia's most visually spectacular frogs in the world. They are between 2.5 and 3 centimetres in length.

Corroboree frogs are the first vertebrates that are able to produce poisonous alkaloids. They do not get the poison via a diet like many other frogs are doing it.

The alkaloid is secreted from the skin as a defence against predation.

Corroboree frogs are living in a small area of South-Eastern New South Wales.

During the breeding season Corroboree frogs live in pools within sphagnum bogs, wet tussock grasslands, and wet heath.

Corroboree frogs generally prefer shallow pools with low water flow and a large surface area. These pools often dry during mid summer which puts the Corroboree frog tadpoles at risk during drought years, as the pools may dry before they can change into young frogs.

Corroboree Frogs have been found under logs and leaf litter in woodlands surrounding breeding habitat so it is likely that they move out of the pools and spend the winter in nearby woodlands.

Corroboree frogs mainly eat small ants and other invertebrates. During winter they eat much less and many individuals don't appear to eat at all.

A single female usually lays between 10 and 40 eggs in a clutch.

A captive Corroboree Frog at Taronga Zoo in Sydney

The Weirdest Looking Toads & Frogs

Brazilian horned frog

The Brazilian Horned Frog, also known as the Ornate Horned Frog or Pac Man Frog, is popular in the pet trade.

These frogs are so popular because they are easy to care for and quite impressive because of their weird and bizarre looks.

It is native to Brazil and other areas in South America. The Brazilian horned frog makes its home in humid rainforests.

They usually live in streams and other bodies of water. Brazilian horned frogs are very aggressive feeders. They capture prey by grabbing anything that ventures too close, killing it with their jaws, and quickly swallowing it.

The Brazilian horned frog's bite is very strong and they will hold on to their prey until it is swallowed or they are forced to let go.

The Brazilian horned frog will eat almost anything, including other frogs that are weaker than themselves.

Let me tell you, these weird looking creatures have a very large appetite, too.

Brazilian horned frogs range in sizes from 5.5 inches (14 centimetres) to almost 9 inches (23 centimetres).

They are multi-colored, often in some combinations of browns, greens and yellows.

They have bumps all over their bodies, which are also quite colorful. They have huge eyes placed on top of their heads. Their stomach is light colored with numerous black spots. They have two horns, triangular in shape, that extend from the eyelids.

Brazilian horned frogs are most commonly found in the rainforests of central and southern Brazil, as well as in northern Argentina.

Goliath frog

Most frogs can fit in the palm of your hand, or even on the tip of your finger. But still the Goliath frog, the world's largest frog, may grow up to 3 feet long when it is stretched out and it can weigh as much as 7 lbs. (3.2 kg).

The Goliath frog's greenish brown color helps it to hide among wet moss-covered rocks in fast-flowing rivers in the dense coastal rainforests of Cameroon and Equatorial Guinea in western Africa.

Unlike most other frogs and toads, Goliath frogs have no vocal sac and therefore they can not make any calls. They mainly eat crabs, but will also eat insects and smaller frogs.

The Goliath frog can live up to 15 years.

Because Goliath frogs live in such a small area of the rainforest, they are highly vulnerable to habitat loss through logging and clearance of forest for agricultural land.

The construction of dams threatens the breeding habitat of these frogs. The frogs have been heavily collected for zoos, breeding programs, research, and pet trade.

Goliath frogs don't breed or survive well if taken in captivity.

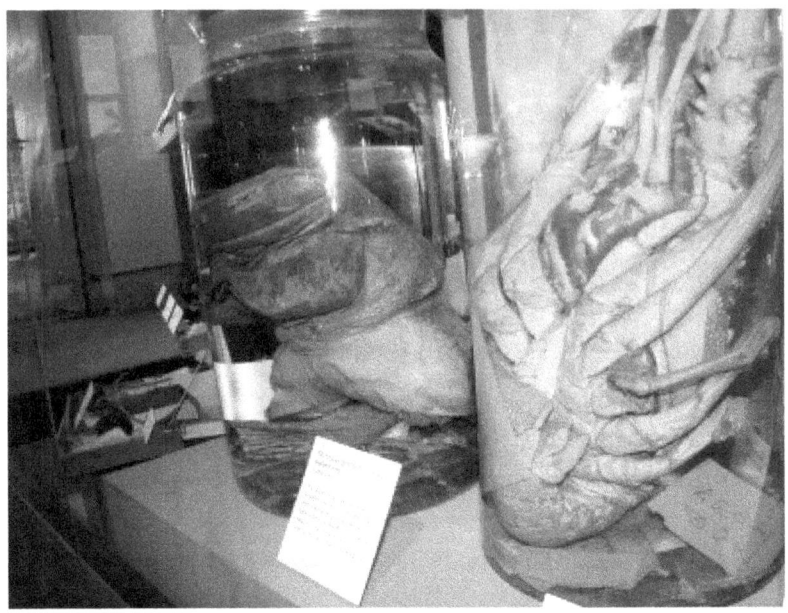

Vietnamese Mossy Frog

The Vietnamese Mossy Frog has a bumpy skin. It looks almost like moss. These frogs can be seen dwelling in mountains and caves.

It is easy for these frogs to hide from enemies because they are blending in with their environment. When they sit in moss, they blend right in with their camouflage hiding tactics!

Turtle Frog

The turtle frog is a very peculiar frog with a body shape that is resembling a small turtle without the shell. The turtle frog's head is very small with reduced eyes. The head of the turtle frog is quite distinct from its body, unlike most other frogs.

The limbs are short but muscular. Like its relative, the sand hill frog, this species burrows forward through the sand. The back color ranges from pink mauve and purple colors to a uniform light to dark browns.

Turtle frogs have been heard calling in the month of July, suggesting regional variation in the timing of reproduction.

Their calling has deep croaks. Female frog lays up to 50 eggs, each measuring as much as 7.5 mm in diameter.

Source: Paul J. Morris

Purple Frog

Purple frogs have been discovered later in 2003. These kinds of frogs spend most of their time being under the ground. They come up to the surface only for laying eggs. Purple frogs breed in the monsoon season.

This beautiful species is facing the threat of deforestation. The forests where the purple frog loves to live have been cleared for plantations of coffee, cardamom and ginger.

Glass Frog

There are many natural wonders in the animal kingdom, perhaps none as unusual as the Glass Frog.

This tiny frog gets its name because of the translucent skin on its underside (and in some species the top as well) that allows you to see its inner organs, right down to its beating heart!

This actually has an advantage for the glass frog. First of all, this glass body makes him very difficult for predators to spot, as he almost becomes a part of the leaf he is sitting on.

If you shine a light on a tree frog at night (if you can find one) all you will see are his eyes and a smudge for his skull.

Glass frogs are very small, the average one being between 1.4 cm and 3 cm (1.2 to 3.0 inches), and they generally live in the rainforests of Central and South America.

Glass frogs are pretty similar in appearance to some green frogs and some tree frogs.

Although they live by streams and rivers, almost all of the glass frogs are arboreal, coming down only to breed.

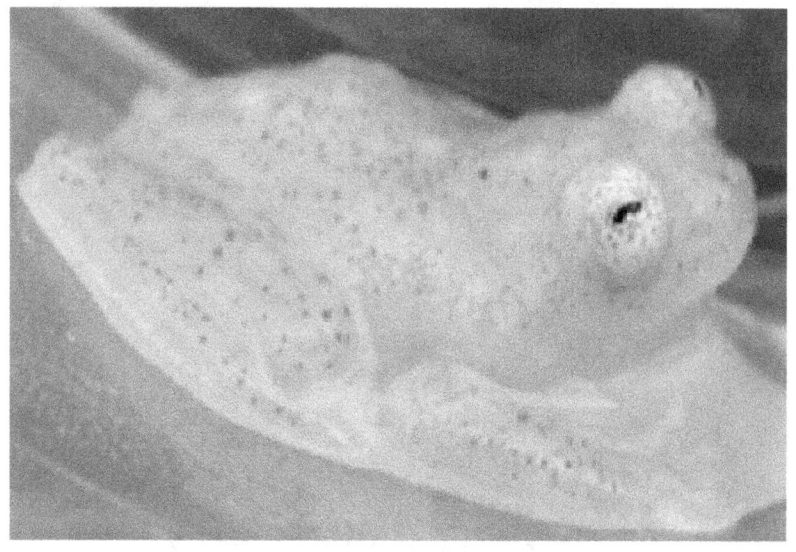

Source: D. F. Cisneros-Heredia

Source: JurriaanH

Source: Froggydarb

Pinocchio Nose Frog

The Pinocchio-nosed frog was discovered recently during a wildlife expedition to Indonesia's remote Foja Mountains.

This long-nosed frog, a tree frog, has a spike on its nose that points upward when the male is calling but deflates and points downward when he is less active.

One thing is for sure, the Pinocchio Nose frog is a very funny and weird looking creature, but researchers and scientists do not know a lot of things about this little creature because its discovery only took place recently by the Conservation International and the National Geographic Society during an expedition in 2008.

This is why there is no picture included for the Pinocchio Nose Frog - Sorry for that!

Once we get an awesome picture that depicts this littel kritter very well we will be updating the book so that you can access the updated content immediately.

Frogs Handsome Enough To Kiss

These are the frogs that are truly handsome enough to kiss

- don't you think...?

Red-Eyed Tree Frog

Many scientists believe that the cute little red-eyed tree frog developed its vivid scarlet peepers to shock predators into at least briefly questioning their meal choice.

These iconic rain-forest amphibians AKA Red-Eyes Tree Frog sleep by day stuck to leaf-bottoms with their eyes closed and body markings covered.

When the are disturbed, they flash their bulging red eyes and reveal their huge, webbed orange feet and bright blue-and-yellow flanks to scare anyone who might harm them off.

Their neon-green bodies may play a similar role in threatening predators and it might be part of their defense coloring system.

Many of the animals that eat red-eyed tree frogs are nocturnal hunters that use keen eyesight to find prey.

The shocking colors of this frog and the neon green color may over-stimulate a predator's eyes, creating a confusing ghost image that remains behind as the frog quickly jumps away into a protected hiding place.

source: Charlesjsharp

Harlequin frogs

source: Axel Kwet

Harlequin frogs are an extremely diverse group of ground-dwelling amphibians. They are found on all continents except Antarctica. Many species of the Harlequin frogs have thick warty skin, but some species are smooth skinned. One unique characteristic of this family is that they have no teeth.

Wood Frog

The Wood Frog's beauty is more subtle that that of its tropical cousins, yet its colors seems to mimic the colour of rocks, bark, and fallen leaves in the forests in which it lives. Its skin resembles wood; hence that is where this frog got its name from.

Wood Frogs go for a long sleep in winter. First they find a place under the leaf litter or in a crack in a log or rock to settle for their winter nap. They'll slowly begin to freeze as soon as the temperature is reaching the freezing point. At the freezing point the frog's blood will stop flowing. The lungs, the heart and the muscles will stop functioning, and ice will fill the body cavity.

These wood frogs will go from frog to frogsicle.

Pretty amazing what these wood frog's bodies can tolerate! Can you imagine their blood and tissues get frozen and then they come out of hibernation as if nothing happened!

Frogs can survive many freeze and thaw events during tough winter times. Yeah, this my friends is one more reason why frogs rock! Don't you agree?

Once the winter is over, they begin to thaw in the warm temperatures of spring and mating time.

Source: Brian Gratwicke

Tiger frog

The Tiger Frog was discovered in 2007 in Southwestern Colombian.
Little is known about the frog except that it is not believed to be toxic.
Rather with its bright colors, the frog seems to be mimicking other poisonous animals to deter predators and to foul them into thinking that tiger frogs are untouchable.
This gorgeous frog is yet another sad example of a threatened frog species. It might face extinction at any point in the future because people are still destroying the forests where these beautiful tiger frogs are living.

White's Tree Frog

The Mexican dumpy frog is also called white's tree frog. These frogs are green, with sticky toes.

They live in forests. They spend their lives on trees. These frogs almost never come down to the ground. These handsome frogs seem to have a perpetual smile that sticks on their faces. They smile as if they knew that they are in good luck and that nothing can happen to them.

White's tree frogs are often kept as pets by humans, but they are happiest when left alone in their native homes and habitats like the woodland and scrub close to the water in the northeast Australia and New Guinea area.

Source LiquidGhoul and Bignoter

Source: Bidgee

Don't I look royal? I bet there is a hidden Prince somewhere! Who knows maybe a Prince appears like magic if you kiss me!

The Absolute Most Bizarre & Weirdest Frogs On Earth

The absolute weirdest frogs on earth are the following...

The gliding leaf frog

The gliding leaf frog is also known as the gliding tree frog or Spurrell's leaf frog.

It can be found in South and Central America.

Their population is decreasing, but not at a rate fast enough to consider them threatened or endangered.

Gliding leaf frogs grow to 3 or 4 inches in length, with the females being slightly larger than the males.

They may grow larger in some habitats than others; for example, Panamanian specimens are reportedly larger than those in Costa Rica.

The gliding leaf frog's colours change from a light yellowish green during the day to a darker green at night. Most of these frogs also have a number of black-bordered white spots on their backs.

They have deep red eyes and fully-webbed feet with large toe pads.

Source: Sandilya Theuerkauf, Wynaad, 2006

The Invisible Frog

Japanese scientists have created an invisible, or at least transparent, frog for medical research so that they may observe its internal organs without dissecting the frog. It will be much less messy that way.

Ahrghhhh - these Japanese folks are a weird ethnic group themselves with all their pop culture and preference for tactile toys that is going on over there in Nippon land!

Anyways, we frogs are always for progress and research.

If the Japanese scientist's research is truly helping the word as a whole to become a better place to live in, we frogs all agree that this migh be a good cause even though it sounds creepy and weird at the same time!

Purple Frog

Source: Karthickbala

Nasikabatrachus sahyadrensis is a frog species that belongs to the family of Sooglossidae.

It can be found in the Western Ghats in India.

This species truly looks weird and has therefore been given various names like the purple frog, the Indian purple frog, and the pignose frog because its nose resembles the nose of a pig.

The body of the Nasikabatrachus sahyadrensis frog appears bloated and robust and bloated. It is relatively rounded compared to other more dorsoventrally and flattened frog species.

Compared to other frogs, the purple frog has a small head and an unusual, pointed snout.

Adult purple frogs are typically dark and colored in a purplish-grey in color.

Male purple frogs are about a third of the length of its female counterparts.

The purple frog is definitely one weird looking creature and it makes a good source of inspiration for one of the next creepy movies that features the purple pig nose frog as the next villain that tries to steal the princess from the kingdom, but in the end everything turns out just peachy because the princess accidentally kisses the monsterous creepy looking creature and the monster turns into a good looking and charming prince!

Don't you love this fairy tale meets horror movie scenario that features purple frog villain monsters, zombies, and maybe even some ninja frog species that are helping the purple frog to escape because it was captured in the beginning of the film. The frogs help with their ninja defense system to free the captivated villain so that it is finally able to free his princess that was captured by the neighbouring enemy kingdom.

The ninja frogs and turtles are all helping out and the purple frog villain monster finally is able to save the princess. The princess experiences one neightmare after the other but accidentally kisses the purple frog and like magic her good looking and charming prince stands in front of her and kisses her back!

I hope you like my creative frog insights and imagignations! Don't you agree that this purple frog would be the perfect character for this kind of fairy tale-monster-ninja movie: "The Purple Frog Monster, the Ninja Frog Defenders & the Princess" or something similar to this.

Even if you do not like my movie idea, I am not really mad at you and I do understand if your taste might be a bit different.

What I do really hope for though is that you have been able to discover and enjoy your discovery. There are so many aspects of us frogs and I truly hope that by now your journey has really helped you shape your own image and opinion about us frogs.

I also hope that you have a better idea of who we truly are and I am sure that by know you can agree that we frogs truly rock!

To give you some more fascinating, intriguing, and curious frog moments and to really prove my point that we frogs rock, I got some more surprises for you in store.

Let's hop over to the next chapter where you will find so many more amazing frog moments...

Some Ultimate Answers To The Question Why Do Frogs Rock?

There is evidence that frogs have roamed the Earth for more than 200 million years, at least as long as the dinosaurs.

The world's largest frog is the goliath frog of West Africa-it can grow to 15 inches and weigh up to 7 pounds.

One of the smallest is the Cuban tree toad, which grows to half an inch long.

While the life spans of frogs in the wild are unknown, frogs in captivity have been known to live more than 20 years.

There are over 6,000 species of frogs worldwide. Scientists continue to search for new ones.

Frogs have excellent night vision and are very sensitive to movement. The bulging eyes of most frogs allow them to see in front, to the sides, and partially behind them. When a frog swallows food, it pulls its eyes down into the roof of its mouth, to help push the food down its throat.

Frogs were the first land animals with vocal cords. Male frogs have vocal sacs-pouches of skin that fill with air. Some frog sounds can be heard from a mile away.

Launched by their long legs, many frogs can leap more than 20 times their body length.

The Costa Rican flying tree frog soars from branch to branch with the help of its feet. Webbing between the frog's fingers and toes extends out, helping the frog glide.

To blend into the environment, the Budgett's frog is muddy brown in colour, while the Vietnamese mossy frog has spotty skin and bumps to make them look like little clumps of moss or lichen.

Many poisonous frogs, such as the golden poison frog and dyeing poison frog, are boldly coloured to warn predators of their dangerous toxic skins.

Although their skins are not toxic, these mimics may gain protection from predators by looking dangerous.

Like all amphibians, frogs are cold-blooded, meaning their body temperatures change with the temperature of their surroundings.

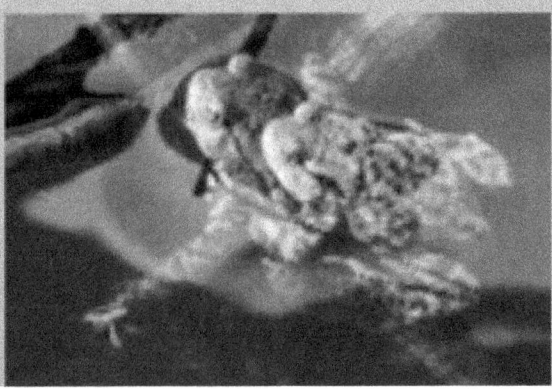

Like all amphibians, frogs are cold-blooded, meaning their body temperatures change with the temperature of their surroundings.

When temperatures drop, some frogs dig burrows underground or in the mud at the bottom of ponds. They hibernate in these burrows until spring, completely still and scarcely breathing.

The wood frog can live north of the Arctic Circle, surviving for weeks with 65 per cent of its body frozen. This frog uses glucose in its blood as a kind of antifreeze that concentrates in its vital organs, protecting them from damage while the rest of the body freezes solid.

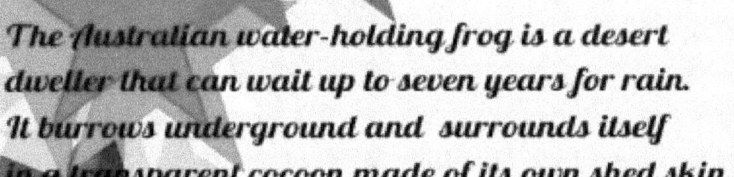

The Australian water-holding frog is a desert dweller that can wait up to seven years for rain. It burrows underground and surrounds itself in a transparent cocoon made of its own shed skin.

Frogs are freshwater creatures, although some frogs such as the Florida leopard frog are able to live in brackish or nearly completely salt waters.

Almost all frogs fertilize the eggs outside of the female's body.

The marsupial frog keeps her eggs in a pouch like a kangaroo. When the eggs hatch into tadpoles, she opens the pouch with her toes and spills them into the water.

Pipa pipa, carries her young embedded in the skin of her back. After mating, the eggs sink gradually into the female's back, and a skin pad forms over the eggs. The developing juvenile frogs are visible inside their pockets for several days before hatching.

They emerge over a period of days, thrusting their head and forelegs out first and then struggling free.

The gastric brooding frog of Australia swallows her fertilized eggs. The tadpoles remain in her stomach for up to eight weeks, finally hopping out of her mouth as little frogs. During the brooding period, gastric secretions cease otherwise she would digest her own offspring.

Among Darwin frogs, it is the male who swallows and stores the developing tadpoles in his vocal sac until juvenile frogs emerge.

Most frogs and toads breathe (and take in moisture) through their skin through a process called cutaneous gas exchange, but they also have lungs with which they breathe. During the time they stay submerged under water or buried in soil (such as during hibernation) they ONLY breathe through their skin.

Frogs' ears are specially "tuned" to absorb the mid-point of the pitch of the call of their particular species. For example, ears of female Spring Peepers are specifically tuned to absorb the mid-point of the pitch of the male Peeper's call.

Spring peepers are one of the first frog species to start calling in the Eastern U.S. and Canada in the spring. These tiny frogs are less than 1 1/4 inches in length. Because they are so small, peepers are nearly impossible to see, yet they can ALWAYS be heard whenever they're singing. The voice of one peeper sounds like a short, high-pitched whistle.
But when a group of spring peepers is calling together they sound like jingle bells on a winter sleigh.

Pacific tree frog is the frog that says "Ribbit!" So it's the one we hear in the background in movies and on TV.
The smallest frogs are the gold frog of Brazil and a frog from Cuba, just discovered in 1996, which doesn't have an English name yet. Both these frogs are less than one centimetre long. Hardly bigger are some of the poison frogs.

The world's tiniest frogs are smaller than a dime, and the largest frog can grow to be longer than a foot and weigh more than 7 pounds!

One gram of the toxin produced by the skin of the golden poison dart frog could kill 100,000 people.

The female Surinam toad lays up to 100 eggs, which are then distributed over her back. Her skin swells around the eggs until they become embedded in a honeycomb-like structure. After 12 to 20 weeks, fully formed young toads emerge by pushing out through the membrane covering the toad's back.

A frog completely sheds its skin about once a week. After it pulls off the old, dead skin, the frog usually eats it.

When Darwin's frog tadpoles hatch, a male frog swallows the tadpoles. He keeps the tiny amphibians in his vocal sac for about 60 days to allow them to grow. He then proceeds to cough up tiny, fully formed frogs.

When a frog swallows its prey, it blinks, which pushes its eyeballs down on top of the mouth to help push the food down its throat.

The wood frog of North America actually freezes in the winter and is reanimated in the spring. When temperatures fall, the wood frog's body begins to shut down, and its breathing, heartbeat and muscle movements stop.
The water in the frog's cells freezes and is replaced with glucose and urea to keep cells from collapsing.

When Darwin's frog tadpoles hatch, a male frog swallows the tadpoles. He keeps the tiny amphibians in his vocal sac for about 60 days to allow them to grow. He then proceeds to cough up tiny, fully formed frogs.

When a frog swallows its prey, it blinks, which pushes its eyeballs down on top of the mouth to help push the food down its throat.

The wood frog of North America actually freezes in the winter and is reanimated in the spring. When temperatures fall, the wood frog's body begins to shut down, and its breathing, heartbeat and muscle movements stop. The water in the frog's cells freezes and is replaced with glucose and urea to keep cells from collapsing.

When there's a thaw, the frog's warms up, its body functions resume and it hops off like nothing ever happened.

A group of birds is called a flock, a group of cattle is called a herd, but a group of frogs is called an army.

The glass frog has translucent skin, so you can see its internal organs, bones and muscles through its skin. You can even observe its heart beating and its stomach digesting food.

There is a frog in Indonesia that has no lungs - it breathes entirely through its skin.

The waxy monkey frog secretes a wax from its neck and uses its legs to rub that wax all over its body. The wax prevents the skin of the frog from drying out in sunlight.

Most frogs have teeth, although usually only on their upper jaw. The teeth are used to hold prey in place until the frog can swallow it.

The biggest frog in the world is the Goliath frog. It lives in West Africa and can measure more than a foot in length and weigh more than 7 pounds - as much as a newborn baby.

There's a type of poison dart frog called the blue-jeans frog. It has a red body with blue legs. It is also sometimes called the strawberry dart frog.

The red-eyed tree frog lays it eggs on the underside of leaves that hang over water. When the eggs hatch, the tadpoles fall into the water below.

Frogs As Pets

By now you have gone through a lot of information about us frogs and this is the point where you might ask yourself if you would like to keep a frog as a pet for yourself!

Here are the most critical questions that you should go through before you engage in such a project.

The first step in owning a pet frog is about understanding the great responsibilities that you as a frog pet owner have to go through. Taking care of a frog can be stressful if you do not know from the beginning of what you are getting yourself into.

You have to take care of the frog on a daily basis and you must be clear on these responsibilities before buying a frog turtle.

Frogs do need a great deal of care.

Depending on which type of frog species you prefer, there are different things to know for each breed.

Make sure to take the following things into consideration.

In order to keep a frog you need at least a 10 gallon aquarium that is suitable for one or two frogs.

If you have more frogs at the same time, increase the tank size.

A terrestrial set-up or a half land/half water set-up is good enough for the frog.

Make sure you have a top for the tanks so that the frog can not escape.

Make sure to use large enough gravel so that the frog does not swallow the gravel.

The water depth should be at least 3-4 inches.

Soil or sphagnum moss is perfect to use.

Make sure you have a water dish that is large enough for the frog to soak in.

Tadpoles can handle an aquarium filled with fresh water.

Add hiding spaces like plants or caves for your frog and/or tadpoles is important.

You can also use a fluorescent lighting source for the frog to bask on and to get its nutrients.

Feeding the frog with earthworms, live crickets, small feeder fish, and mealworms is a good diet for a green frog, for example.

You can use Vitamin D3 to powder the food of your frog.

You can get the powder from your local pet store.

Make sure to never catch food out in the wild to feed to your froggy.

Wild food may contain harmful chemicals and pesticides that might harm and even kill your frog.

These are just a few basic tips that will help you determine your frog's needs.

Each specific breed of frog is different. Make sure to inform yourself about every angle that you need to be aware of before getting the frog.

Once you are aware of what a frog needs and its basic needs, make sure to write them down which makes this whole process more real and feasible.

Think about your responsibilities as a frog owner like what are you going to do with the frog when you leave for the weekend or for a long vacation and in case your frog gets sick.

Make sure to discuss your project with your parents first and look at the financial aspect as well. You can make a list of things that you need to buy one time and a list of things that you need to buy on a weekly or daily basis like food for the frog. If you can not finance the basic needs of a frog, it makes no sense to keep a pet because it will not be a happy pet without the necessary care.

If you do not have enough money to buy proper food, your frog will not be able to develop into a healthy frog because it lacks a proper nutrition.

In this case you might find a way how to earn some of your own money to make sure you can provide everything that a frog needs or you can go to the zoo and admire the beauty of us frogs in an environment that has the funds to care for us frogs so that we can develop into some beautiful and self-sustainable creatures.

At the zoo everyone has the chance to admire us beautiful creatures. The zoo provides a great opportunity for everyone who loves animals and who can not keep his or her favorite animal at home.

Guess what!

There are even stranger and weirder animals than us frogs that you can visit at the zoo!

Make sure to come up with a wise decision if you can or can not keep a pet frog and don't be sad if you can't because there are so many other opportunities for you that you can take into consideration to discover more about us, to help, and to support us.

One thing is for sure we do not love to be kept in a tiny space with no food and no room for development. In general, we do not like to be kept in a caged zoo neither because who likes to be kept and taken under surveillance all day long?

Living at the zoo, however, is still better than in a tiny tank where there is no space at all.

Living in our natural habitat around the globe is where we are most happy and develop best. There are many risks that we face there and it is a tough fight for us. Only the strongest survive out there because out in the nature by ourselves we have to face many obstacles on a daily basis.

Having to imagine that one of us has to live in a cage that provides no space at all and without the proper food is an even creepier thought.

This is the reason why you really should make sure to come up with a wise decision that is in favor of us frogs and hopefully you will appreciate us for who we are when you are making your decision.

Giving us the proper treatment is the basis for a co-existence between human being and us frogs.

Before you go ahead with any frog pet project, please make sure you consider every aspect and come to a fair judgement.

We need proper treatment and food on a daily basis. Sometimes we might get sick and we need medical care.

Thanks for considering every aspect about us before taking your final decision so that we can develop into a beautiful and happy frog that you can be proud of and admire!

Is The Future Of Frogs In Danger?

The Golden toad of Monteverde, Costa Rica, was among the first casualties of amphibian declines.
Formerly abundant, it was last seen in 1989.

Now that you hopefully can appreciate us and our various species, you might be interested in some more serious stuff that concerns our future and your future at the same time because we all live on the same planet and we need to make sure that we support each other!

Did you know that some of the frog species are declining and even endangered at the hand of humans?

Yes, it is true and we are very sad about it because we frogs have come such a long way.

Sadly, the fact is that we frogs and other endangered animals face many dangers as we are living around the world today. These are artificial dangers created by human greed and power.

Source: Brian Gratwicke from DC, USA

Since the 80s, declines in our amphibian populations are happening. This decline of us frog species includes mass localized extinctions and population crashes that have been noted from locations all over the globe.

Some of our frog species declines are perceived as one of the most critical threats to global biodiversity.

Several causes are believed to be involved, including human habitat destruction and modification, diseases, exploitation, pollution with pesticides and other harmful chemicals, introduced species, and increased ultraviolet-B radiation (UV-B radiation).

Our frog populations have declined significantly since the 50s. More than one third of species are considered to be threatened with extinction.

Over 120 of our frog species are believed to have become extinct since the 80s.

The number of malformations among us frogs is on the rise.

Sadly enough, we frogs are valued as food items by human beings and are thretened by these human predators on a constant basis.

We frogs have been known to survive and adapt throughout evolution and we are creatures that are well-adapted to nature and our habitats, but we are not able to adapt to artificial human activities that harm us frogs like deforestation, logging, and the pollution of the environment.

In nature, we frogs are facing a constant host of life and death obstacles. We are fighting a daily survival struggle against animal and human predators.

Animals that eat frogs for snacks include snakes, lizards, birds, and various small animals like hedgehogs. Even under water we frogs can not be safe from hungry sharp toothed fish, swimming mammals like water shrews, and even diving birds!

As if that wasn't bad enough, we frogs even have to watch out for other hungry frogs because there are even frogs that eat other frogs.

Because there are so many bad guys to watch out for, we frogs and toads have come up with a large variety of forms of protection.

To understand what really threatens the survival of our population, you must look at the actions of humans and what humans do to our beautiful natural habitats.

These are the things that harm us most:

Predators, other frog competitors, pollution, pesticide use, and over-harvesting. However, many amphibian declines or extinctions have occurred in pristine habitats where the above effects are not likely to occur. The causes of these declines are complex, but many can be attributed to emerging diseases, climate change, increased ultraviolet-B radiation, or long-distance transmission of chemical contaminants by wind.

Artificial lighting has been suggested as another potential cause. Insects are attracted to lights making them scarcer within our amphibian habitats.

Habitat modifications and fragmentations or complete destructions are one of the most dramatic issues affecting us amphibian species worldwide. As amphibians generally need aquatic and terrestrial habitats to survive, threats to either habitat can affect our populations. Hence, amphibians may be more vulnerable to habitat modification than organisms that only require one habitat type. Large scale climate changes may further be modifying aquatic habitats, preventing us amphibians from spawning altogether.

There is evidence of chemical pollutants causing our frog developmental deformities (extra limbs, or malformed eyes).

Pollutants have varying effects on us frogs. Some alter the central nervous system; others like atrazine cause a disruption in the production and secretion of hormones. Experimental studies have also shown that exposure to commonly used herbicides such as glyphosate or insecticides such as malathion or carbaryl greatly increase mortality of us tadpoles.

Some recent evidence points to ozone as a possible contributing factor to the worldwide decline of us amphibians, too.

Like many other organisms, increasing ultraviolet-B (UVB radiation) due to stratospheric ozone depletion and other factors may harm the DNA of us amphibians, particularly our eggs.

The amount of damage depends upon the life stage, the species type and other environmental parameters.

New evidence has shown global warming to also be capable of directly degrading our friends the toads' bodies and body conditions and survivorship is very slim.

Additionally, the phenomenon often colludes with landscape alterations, pollution of various types, and species invasions to effect the extinction of us amphibians.

A number of diseases have been related to declines in populations of us amphibians.

A study showed that high levels of nutrients used in ranching and farming has caused frog deformities in lakes and ponds across North America causing extra limbs, missing limbs, and other severe malformations including five or six extra legs or even no limbs at all.

Non-native predators and competitors have also been found to affect the viability of us frogs in our habitats. The mountain yellow-legged frog which typically inhabits the Sierra Nevada lakes has seen a decline in numbers due to stocking of non-native fish like trout for recreational fishing purposes.

The developing tadpoles and froglets fall prey to trout fish in very large numbers.

We frogs and toads are highly vocal, and our reproductive behaviour often involves the use of vocalizations. There have been suggestions that increased noise levels caused by human activities may be contributing to our declines, too.

Putting everything into perspective, humans and their unnatural activities are still our biggest threat and humans can really hurt us by interfering with every stage of our life cycle.

This is why we need your help to get our population numbers back to normal.

So what can humans do to protect us, you may ask?

One positive thing that has evolved and that is in place to protect our rights is the fact that some human beings like you have been showing initiative for our cause of decline.

In the beginning of 2007, scientists and experts worldwide met in Atlanta, U.S.. They formed a group called the Amphibian Ark to help save more than 6,000 species of us lovely amphibians from disappearing. They also started running captive breeding programs for us amphibians.

Conservation efforts have also been created by some organizations such as the World Wildlife Fund to help further studies on why we frogs go through extinction and to help educate people on the issue at hand and Amphibian Conservation Alliance (ACA).

Areas with noticed frog extinctions, like Australia, have few policies that have been created to prevent the extinction of these species. Local initiatives have been placed where conscious efforts to decrease global warming will also turn into a conscious effort towards saving us frogs.

In South America, where there is also an increased decline of amphibian populations, there is no set policy to try to save us frogs. Some suggestions would include getting entire governments to place a set of rules and institutions as a source of guidelines that local governments have to abide by.

We are peaceful and in general non harmful animals if we are not groped and grabbed by humans.

We also add natural beauty to the earth, the ponds, the trees, and the forests.

We even help humans catch nasty flies.

There is one difference though. We do not kill humans if they do not attack us first, but humans unintentionally or intentionally might harm and kill us!

We are smart, too, because otherwise we would not have been able to survive for millions of years until today.

Once we have reached adulthood and luckily for those who make it, we won't be a prey so easily because some of us really have learned to develop some awesome ninja defense mechanisms over the years. We have survived until today because we were smart and wise enough to adapt through evolution. Evolution has taught us how to protect ourselves from predators over the years.

As you have learned by now some of our frog species are pretty poisonous towards any predator.

However, not all of us are as strong and poisonous as the golden poison dart frog, for example, so we need your help in order to survive. Humans can protect us and give us a safe environment were we can live in a happy and balanced self sustained life.

In captivity, many of us frog species and toads, can live for surprisingly very long times. The average is somewhere between four and fifteen years.

If you have not read the previous chapter yet, please make sure to read it because this will help you understand why we are truly awesome creatures and why you must absolutely help us survive!

Please refer to the next chapter "Please Help Us" where you can see how your initiative might save our species…

Help Us!

We frogs do live a longer lifespan if we live in a protected environment like a zoo or a protected home. Did you know that we can reach the age of 15 years and more if we are in a captivated and protected environment?

In general we are a very friendly species if we are not attacked. Otherwise some of us can turn into pretty poisonous creatures to defend themselves.

To protect us some responsible human beings have developed protection programs for us so that we can live a peaceful life in harmony.

However, if we frogs live in the wild, we do fear humans who are ignorant of our space and natural habitats.

Today, more and more of us frogs are captivated in zoos around the globe and we are taken care of via some cool humans and their protection programs. These humans show initiative for our case.

It is very sad that we need such protection programs as opposed to being able to survive ourselves in the wild nature like the rules of mother nature are suggesting it.

However, we are not capable to follow mother nature's law because of some ignorant human beings who harm and kill us and we are therefore very thankful for these protected places that have been created for us and for our survival.

Some humans do a lot to help us and to make sure that we frogs are well taken care of.

Thanks to all of those people who are actively helping us through their initiatives.

On the other side, there are other humans who can truly be a serious threat to us frogs.

We fear humans who do not respect our freedom and rights. We fear the people who keep hunting us because they think we taste good or other weird reasons. We fear the people who hunt us down for their own benefits and profit.

The best way to help us frogs is by not consuming us as food and by showing some initiative for our cause.

Conservation efforts and breeding programs are in place to restore our population to a normal level.

Today there are animal rights and laws in place that makes hunting for us and destructing our habitats an illegal act.

Thanks for your engagement and initiative in putting out this message to everyone you know because you can make a huge difference! If everybody will put out the message like you do, our terrible endangered condition that we live in today might change for the better tomorrow!

We love peace, we are peaceful animals and we enjoy our happiness!

If you love us frogs, too, make sure to defend us against these animal haters who do not seem to care about us and who hunt us down for their own benfits and money gains.

Thanks for sharing the message and thanks for being our fan and friend!

…and make sure to put out this message to others because we are an endangered species and we need Your HELP!

Everybody around the planet needs to get this message!

About the Publisher

InfinitYou is a hybrid general interest trade publisher. One of the first of its kind InfinitYou publishes physical books, electronic books, and audiobooks in various genres. Our publications are meant to educate, edify and entertain readers of all walks of life from babies to the elderly. Home to more than twenty imprints such as Infinit Baby, Infinit Kids, Infinit Girl, Infinit Boy, Infinit Coloring, Infinit Swear Words, Infinit Activities, Infinit Productivity, Infinit Cat, Infinit Dog, Infinit Love, Infinit Family, Infinit Survival, Infinit Health, Infinit Beauty, Infinit Spirituality, Infinit Lifestyle, Infinit Wealth, Infinit Romance, and lots more.

www.ingramcontent.com/pod-product-compliance
Lightning Source LLC
LaVergne TN
LVHW011936070526
838202LV00054B/4680